WITHDRAWN by
Memphis Public Library

Let's Write! K-1

Thinking, Reading, Writing, Speaking and Listening Activities to Promote Creative Expression

Written by Robynne Eagan and Tracey Ann Schofield

Illustrated by Mary Galan Rojas

Teaching & Learning Company

1204 Buchanan St., P.O. Box 10
Carthage, IL 62321-0010

Cover design by Jennifer Little

Copyright © 1999, Teaching & Learning Company

ISBN No. 1-57310-201-6

Printing No. 987654321

Teaching & Learning Company
1204 Buchanan St., P.O. Box 10
Carthage, IL 62321-0010

The purchase of this book entitles teachers to make copies for use in their individual classrooms only. This book, or any part of it, may not be reproduced in any form for any other purposes without prior written permission from the Teaching & Learning Company. It is strictly prohibited to reproduce any part of this book for an entire school or school district, or for commercial resale.

All rights reserved. Printed in the United States of America.

This book belongs to

_____

Dedications

To all the young children, particularly my own, who made me see and believe in the value of such a book.

            Tracey

To my grandmothers: Edith Cochrane and Elizabeth Johnson, for all of the stories over the years.

            Robynne

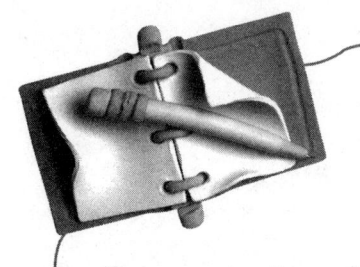

Table of

Communicating with Parents 7
Observing, Assessing and Evaluating
    Language Development 8
Observing and Assessing Young Writers . 9

Chapter 1: Letters, Letters, Everywhere

Letter-Making Center 11
A Letter a Day 12
Alphabet Accomplishment Train 13
My Letter Bead Chain 14
Letter Hunt 15
Twist and Shout 16
Musical Letters 17
Name Bingo 19
The Mechanics of Printing 20
Early Letter-Making Tasks 21
Pre-Printing Exercise Strips 22
Progress Through Printing 23
Making Letters 24
Uppercase Alphabet 25
Lowercase Alphabet 27
Upper/Lowercase Alphabet 29

Chapter 2: Sounds, Sounds, They're All Around!

Oral Language Experience 32
Let's Listen! 33
What Would Happen If . . . ? 34
Listen for the Letter 35
Leaping Letters 36
Letter Links 37

Broken Telephone 38
Alliteration Name Game 39
Musical Associations 41
Clowning Around with Language 43
Clowning Around-Abouts Cut-Outs 44
Poetry Power .46
   Which Word Doesn't Belong? 46
   What Is a Rhyming Word? 46
   Give It a Try! 46
   What Is a Poem? 47
   Share a Poem 47
   Let's Take a Look 47

Chapter 3: World of Words

Pick a Card 49
Word Tag 50
Alphabet Excursions 51
Pass the Package 53
Alphabooks 54
Signs, Symbols, Labels and Logos 55
The Sorting Game 57
Wish Lists 58
Create a Recipe 59
Emotion Promotion 61
Happy Face/Sad Face Cut-Outs 62
Sensational Seasons 63
Sensational Seasons Cut-Outs 64
Learning to Spell 65
Early Spelling Strategies 66
Take-a-Try 67
My Word Treasure Chest 68
Word Gem Cut-Outs 69

Contents

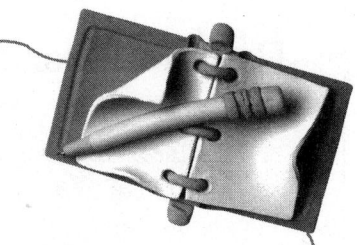

Chapter 4: Ready to Write
Learning to Write 71
Strategies for Teaching
  Early Writing Skills 72
Kindergarten Writing Center 73
Grade 1 Writing Center 74
Capitalization 75
One or More? 76
Punctuation Playtime 77
Punctuation Playtime Cut-Outs 79
Simple Sign-Ins 80
Make a Greeting Card 81
Word Wishes 82
Good News/Bad News 83
Writing Folder 84
Writing Folder Copy Page 85
Sharing 86
Publish Your Work 87

Chapter 5: Story Makers
From Reading to Writing 89
Stories, Stories, Everywhere! 90
Invite a Storyteller 91
Circle Stories 92
Say It with Pictures 93
Picture Card Story Sequencers 94
Picture Card Story Cut-Outs 95
Story Box 98
Scribe a Story 99
Silly Sentences 100
Silly Sentences Flip-Up Book 101
Silly Sentences Sample Grid 102
Story Lovers' Club 103

Chapter 6: Just for Fun
Imagination Station 112
Spread the News 113
The Magic Looking Glass 115
The Magic Looking Glass Copy Page . 116
What Will Grow from the Magic Beans? 117
Magic Beans Copy Page 118
Who Wore These? 119
What's Inside? 120
What Would They Say? 121
BYOS (Bring Your Own Senses) Party 122

Appendix
Kindergarten Writing Readiness
  Assessment Form 124
Grade 1 Writing Assessment Form . . 126
Stages of Writing Development
  Checklist 128

Dear Teacher or Parent,

Children love language. As educators, we can nurture this natural affinity and augment it with an understanding of the mechanics of written expression to help children become enthusiastic, motivated and competent writers. But the real magic begins when we sprinkle a liberal dose of creative inspiration over the common curriculum and kids begin to put words on paper—not because they have to write, but because they want to write!

The first in the Let's Write! creative writing series, *Let's Write! K-1*, is the young child's window to the wonderful world of written communication. Packed with motivational ideas, innovative teaching suggestions, fun-filled writing games and activities and developmental observation and assessment checklists, *Let's Write!* offers educators a fresh approach to creative writing that fascinates young children and facilitates learning.

Let's Write! K-1 incorporates the interdisciplinary skills of communication—thinking, reading, writing, speaking and listening—in an exciting, new creative writing program that combines the mechanics of writing with the joy of creative expression. From the earliest stages of language development and letter recognition to the point where kids are able to put words to work, *Let's Write!* helps young children discover the exhilaration of writing and the power of the written word.

By promoting a creative learning environment and using tools such as *Let's Write!* to teach children at all levels the art of transcribing their ideas into writing, educators are giving a gift that lasts a lifetime.

Each book in the Let's Write! series is designed to expose young writers to the wonder of words and the magic of language. The books, which provide educators with a collection of exciting activities that introduce and expand on reading, writing and expressive concepts for three targeted developmental levels, can stand alone as creative writing units or be used in combination to supplement the language curriculum.

Sincerely,

Robynne   Tracey

Robynne Eagan and Tracey Ann Schofield

Communicating with Parents

Parental involvement in the early grades may be the key to success that will make a good writing program a great writing program.

Focus your communications with parents on the progress and goals established by and for the particular child. Keep parents informed about skills their child is learning and what goals and expectations you have for this student. Let parents know how they can help. Young writers will need lots of practice, reinforcement and encouragement as they come to make sense of the big, wide world of the printed word.

Communicate with parents by way of formal written communications, daily notes in a communication book, formal presentations and meetings, scheduled parent/teacher conferences and informal drop-in sessions throughout the year.

Help parents to focus on the progress their child is making.

Observing, Assessing and Evaluating Language Development

Language development encompasses expectations in areas of written, oral and visual communication. A developmentally appropriate language program is essential for young learners. Familiarize yourself with the predictable range of abilities for this age group and focus on each child's current developmental stage. Careful observation and assessment will guide educators in the development of an appropriate language program.

Evaluation and assessment can be viewed as extensions of the writing process and used as tools to further enhance a young writer's growth. Assess children according to the expectations outlined for their grade level. Use prescribed resources and assessment criteria along with professional judgment to assess a child's degree of mastery of specific knowledge and skills.

Assess and evaluate with respect and a positive attitude. Assessments and evaluations should be a part of the writing process, but bear in mind that young authors need to feel secure about their writing–even if it needs work!

Help young writers recognize and take pride in their accomplishments, as they become aware of their strengths and weaknesses.

knowledge: facts, concepts, ideas, vocabulary and stories possessed and understood by an individual

skill: ability to perform a specific task that can be learned, observed and evaluated

Observing and Assessing Young Writers

There are several methods for systematically observing young writers. A combination of these methods will provide a good basis for understanding individual developmental levels. Master one method at a time and build a repertoire of assessment tools that work best for you. You can use a combination of systematic observation assessment techniques during any language activity.

Stages of Development Forms
Create a page to outline the various stages of predictable language development. Graphs, checklists or observational comments can be incorporated into this form.

Anecdotal Comments
Carry a clipboard and jot down notes, dates, key points that will help you to recall the point, record new skills, mastery or a skill as you observe children in various activities. Collect your observations in notebooks or personal anecdotal reporting pages. These notes will be useful at evaluation time, and parents will appreciate snapshots of their child in action.

Observation Checklist
Develop observation forms to be used for individuals engaged in a particular activity. Create a list of definite skills and development that you expect this activity to demonstrate and teach.

_____'s
Anecdotal Report

Date	Observation

Writing Center Activity Checklist

Name: _____

Date: _____

Observations

☐ demonstrates skill with writing tools

☐ demonstrates creativity in written work

☐ combines print and pictures to express ideas

☐ makes use of various strategies to spell words

Chapter 1

Letters, Letters, Everywhere

Letter-Making Center

Design a letter-making center that incorporates these letter-learning activities.

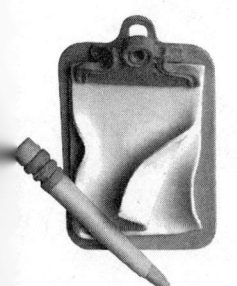

Make a sign featuring a neatly printed model letter to act as a guide for young letter makers.

Supplies

- ✓ playdough or clay and a sample letter "sculpture" model
- ✓ cut-out letters with paste and stick-on glitter, tiny pasta, beads, sequins, rice, sand, cotton, eggshells, etc.
- ✓ construction paper and markers, pencils, pens, crayons, pastels or paint and paintbrushes
- ✓ heavy gauge paper and squeeze-on paints
- ✓ finger paint, finger paint trays (purchased or made) and cover-ups
- ✓ colored sand in a tray for nonpermanent letter creations
- ✓ cookie dough, letter-shaped cookie cutters and volunteer bakers
- ✓ a copy sheet with the letter to be traced and colored
- ✓ construction paper, paste and tissue to be torn, crumpled and pasted to form the letter shape
- ✓ letter scrap books–add and decorate a letter each day to make an alphabet book
- ✓ magazines and newspapers for a letter search; scissors, paste and mural paper for making a letter collage
- ✓ letter stamps and ink pads

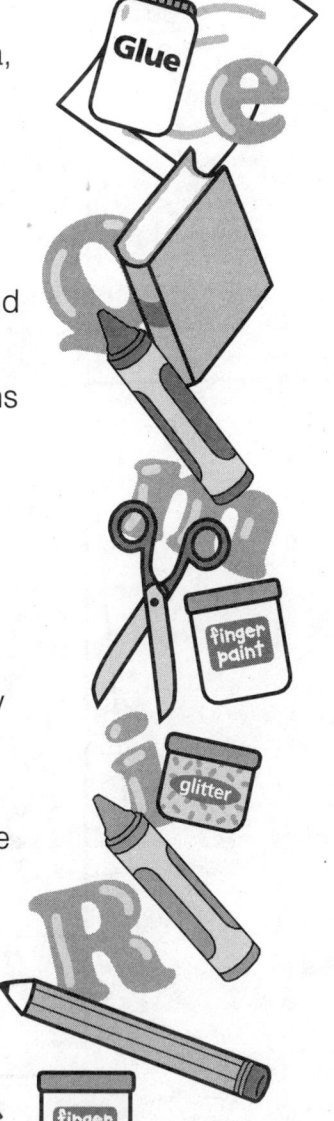

A Letter a Day

The "Letter a Day" approach offers children a simple, focused program that ensures that all letters are introduced and reinforced.

Send home a class calendar that shows the "letter of the day." Children can wear colors or bring snacks that start with the letter on the given day.

Focus on one letter each day for four days, and then review all four letters on the fifth day for reinforcement.

It is very important for children to hear the sound, make the sound and listen for the sound as they associate it with the printed representation.

Ask some questions to create associations. What does this letter look like to you? Where have you seen this letter before?

S	M	T	W	T	F	S
	1 a	2 b	3 c	4 d	5 abcd	6
7	8 e	9 f	10 g	11 h	12 efgh	13
14	15 i	16 j	17 k	18 l	19 ijkl	20
21	22 m	23 n	24 o	25 p	26 mnop	27
28	29 q	30 r	31 s			

March

Alphabet Accomplishment Train

Make tracks to learn letters with lettered rail cars. When a new letter is introduced, print it on a rail car. Display these letters around the classroom and add a new rail car each time a new letter is introduced.

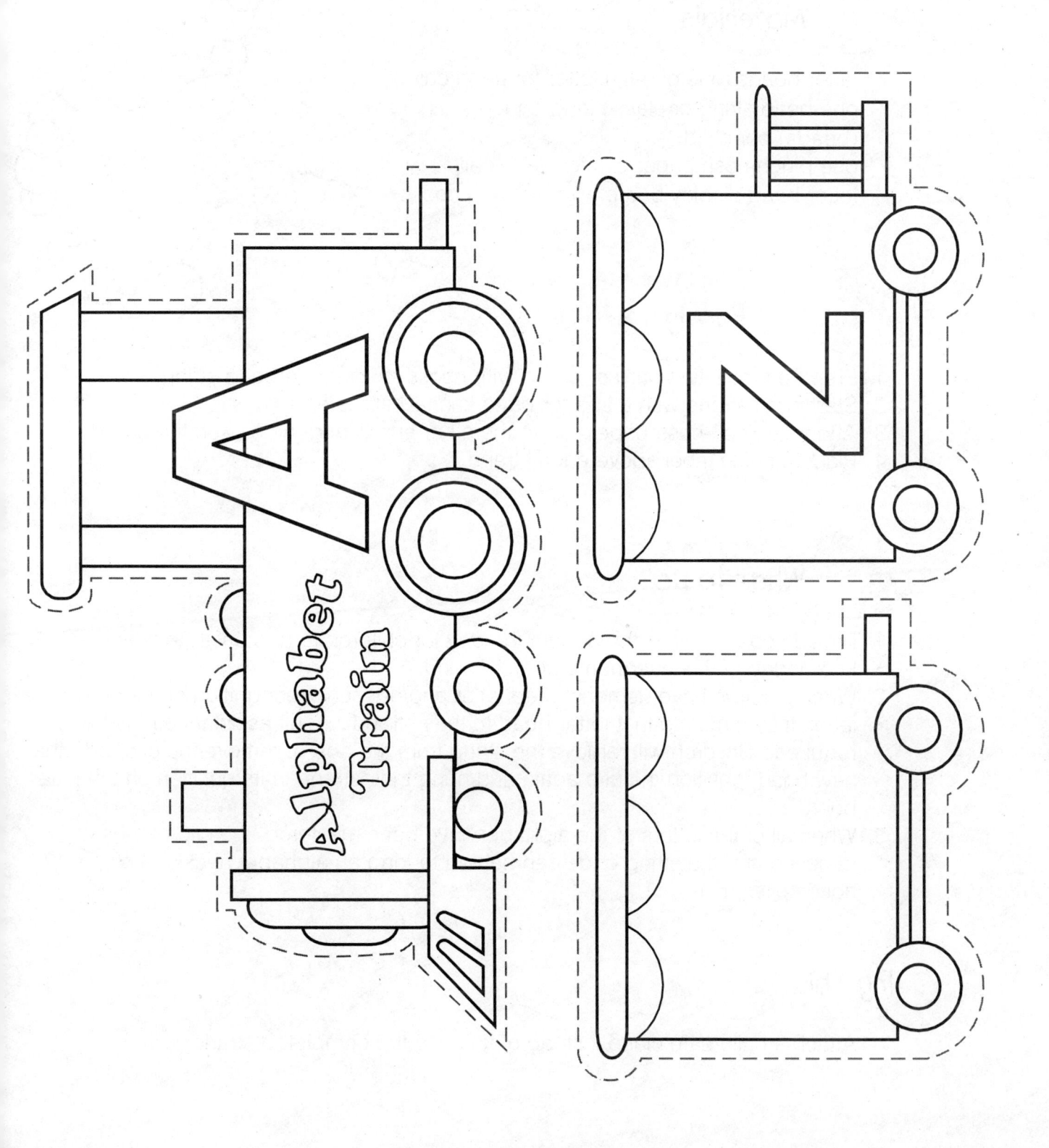

My Letter Bead Chain

A kid-friendly way to keep track of letter and sound recognition skills!

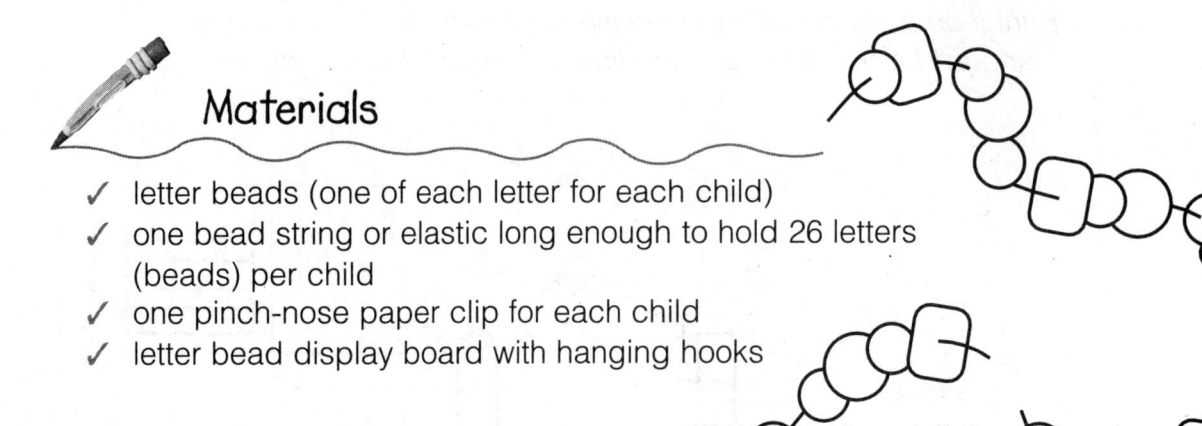

Materials

- ✓ letter beads (one of each letter for each child)
- ✓ one bead string or elastic long enough to hold 26 letters (beads) per child
- ✓ one pinch-nose paper clip for each child
- ✓ letter bead display board with hanging hooks

Get Ready

1. Prepare a bulletin board or board with hooks to hang the bead strings.
2. Start each strand with a spacer bead knotted at the end.
3. Attach a pinch-nose paper clip to the other end. Hang the clip on the board.
4. Place a name label above each strand.

What to Do

1. Provide opportunities throughout the day for children to demonstrate their knowledge of the letter name and/or sound.
2. When children have demonstrated letter and/or sound recognition of the new letter, they may add that letter bead to their strand. Adult assistance may be required. Children will remove the string from the board, remove the clip, add the new bead, position the clip again and hang their strand in its position on the letter board.
3. When all of the letters of the alphabet have been mastered, the clip can be removed and the string ends can be tied to form an alphabet necklace of accomplishment.

Try This

- ✓ Attach a child-safe clasp instead of knotting the completed strand.

Name _____

Letter Hunt

This scavenger hunt reinforces letter recognition and improves fine motor skills.

Make sure each "letter hunter" has a Letter Hunter sheet and a handful of crayons. Have the children search the classroom for the letters on their bears. Each time a child finds a new letter, she can color the bear that corresponds to that letter.

TLC10201 Copyright © Teaching & Learning Company, Carthage, IL 62321-0010

Twist and Shout

A letter-recognition game for one to three players!

Materials

- large spinner marked with letters
- large vinyl mat (about 4' x 8' [1.2 x 2.4 m]) marked with rows of letters

Get Ready

Prepare the child-size gameboard by marking letters in rows along the board with indelible marker and/or adhesive-backed sticker material cut into letter shapes. Space letters about 12" (.30 m) apart. Use only four different letters in each game.

How to Play

1. Choose one child to spin and shout out the indicated letter. Two or more players can twist around the letters. Players should remove their footwear. If you find the children are sliding too much, they can remove their socks as well.
2. The "spinner" will spin the indicator and call out the letter that is indicated on the board.
3. Players must put one foot on the called letter.
4. Spinner spins and calls out another letter and players place their other foot on the new letter.
5. On the next spin players move one foot to the called letter. This moving of feet continues until players find themselves tangled or all played out!

Try This

- More advanced players may use hands and feet for a more challenging game.

Musical Letters

A great game for kindergarten learners that combines music and movement and promotes turn taking, role playing and letter recognition by sight and sound.

Materials

- one set of laminated alphabet cards (pages 25-30)
- cassette recorder or CD player and music cassette or CD (children's tunes and variations of the alphabet song are most appropriate)

How to Play

1. Begin this game with a simple review of the letter names or sounds. As you place the laminated alphabet cards, letter-side up, in a circle on the floor, hold up each letter and have the group repeat the letter name and sound. (The letters can be arranged in alphabetical order or distributed randomly. At times, you might want to use a multiple laminated letter cards for a specific letter. This will help to reinforce learning when you are focusing your classroom teaching on a particular letter.)
2. Have the children walk around the perimeter of the circle and freeze when the music stops. (Try a few practice runs before the game.)
3. Call out a letter (and/or write it on the board).
4. Have the children look at the letter(s) at their feet.
5. The child closest to the letter called picks up the card and steps into the middle of the circle, displaying the card for her classmates.
6. The other children circle the child in the middle singing "The Musical Letter Song" (to the tune of "The Farmer in the Dell").

    She/He found the letter "A"
    She/He found the letter "A"
    Hi ho the dairy O
    She/He found the letter "A."

7. The child replaces the letter in its original spot and rejoins the circle.
8. Play continues as before.

Try This

- ✓ Announce (and/or draw) the letter in advance of the music. The children circle the alphabet while the music plays, searching for the letter called. When the music stops, play continues as before.

- ✓ Place the letters facedown on the floor. When the music stops, each child turns over the letter closest to him. If a child uncovers the letter called, he steps into the middle of the circle. The other players return their letters to the floor, facedown, and play continues as above.

- ✓ Have the child in the circle remain in the middle and call the next letter.

- ✓ Call letters in a particular order to spell a word. At the end of each round, the child with the letter steps out of the circle and joins the other children with letters, forming a line from left to right. When the word is complete, the children reenter the circle, and the others circle the group singing the song and substituting the complete word for individual letters.
  Note: Word must not use duplicate letters.

- ✓ When the music stops, have all the children move to the letter called.

- ✓ Focus the game on letter sounds versus letter names or use a combination of the two.

- ✓ Tape laminated letters on carpet sample mats. For variety, paint letters on non-slip vinyl or foam rubber mats or use large foam rubber letters instead of laminated alphabet cards.

- ✓ Try this game outdoors in good weather. Use laminated letter cards on grass, or chalk the letters onto the pavement.

Name Bingo

Materials

- ✓ one set of laminated alphabet pages
- ✓ paper
- ✓ scissors
- ✓ marker
- ✓ bingo chips (can be any kind of game marker)

How to Play

1. Make a Name Bingo card for every child in the class. (You can use full names or first names only.) To make cards, cut paper into strips. Write each child's name horizontally on one of these paper strips. Draw a vertical line between each letter, roughly dividing the strip into squares.
2. Give each child his name strip and enough bingo chips to cover each letter.
3. Spread the laminated cards facedown on the table.
4. Explain to the children that you will be picking up different laminated cards and calling out the letters that appear on them. Their job is to look for those letters on their card and cover each one with a bingo chip. When every letter of their name is covered with a chip–when their name card is "full"–they can all out, "bingo!" and win the game.
5. With the children seated at their desks, pick a laminated card, call out the letter that is on it and place the letter card on the chalkboard ledge for reference and the end-of-game check.
6. Play continues until a child calls, "bingo!"
7. Ask the winner to call out the letters on her card. As each letter is called, check that it is on the chalkboard ledge. If all the letters have been called, declare the child the winner and name her the next Bingo Master. This child then draws and calls the letters for the next game.

The Mechanics of Printing

The Magical Symbols

Facilitate an awareness and excitement about print long before children are ready to begin writing. When early learners are introduced to the symbols of print, they are very excited about cracking the code of the written language. Visual romps through the alphabet are followed by the learning of letter names, sounds and, in time, replicating these symbols on their own. A child who develops mastery over these symbols has the tools to begin writing.

How Can I Teach Children to Make Letters?

A child's first experiences with print should generate interest and enjoyment that will last a lifetime. Provide a range of activities to fascinate, challenge and develop competence.

Seize opportunities to teach letter recognition and letter making, but do not push children beyond their capabilities. Prepare tasks that will accommodate the great variance of fine motor abilities within any given group.

Early Letter-Making Tasks

Hands-on experience with letter models offers opportunities for developmentally appropriate letter recognition and letter-making tasks.

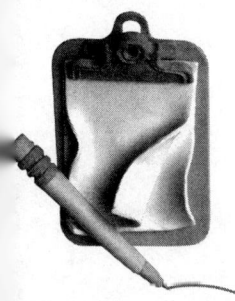

Provide opportunities for the children to...

...make letters with their hands

- ✓ in sand or mud
- ✓ in the snow
- ✓ with rolls of modeling clay
- ✓ with cookie dough
- ✓ with finger paint

...trace letters using writing tools

- ✓ stencils
- ✓ photocopies
- ✓ letters on a chalkboard and colored chalk

...copy model letters using these tools

- ✓ paper and large crayons, markers and primary and fine pencils
- ✓ paper, paintbrushes and paint

Try This

- ✓ Use of pencil grips may be helpful for some children.
- ✓ Research has shown that some children learn best when exposed to three-dimensional models.

Pre-Printing Exercise Strips

Trace and copy the shapes.

squiggle	horizontal line	vertical line
vertical lines side by side	box	X
box with an X inside	S shape	circle
U shape	mountains (m and n)	

Progress Through Printing

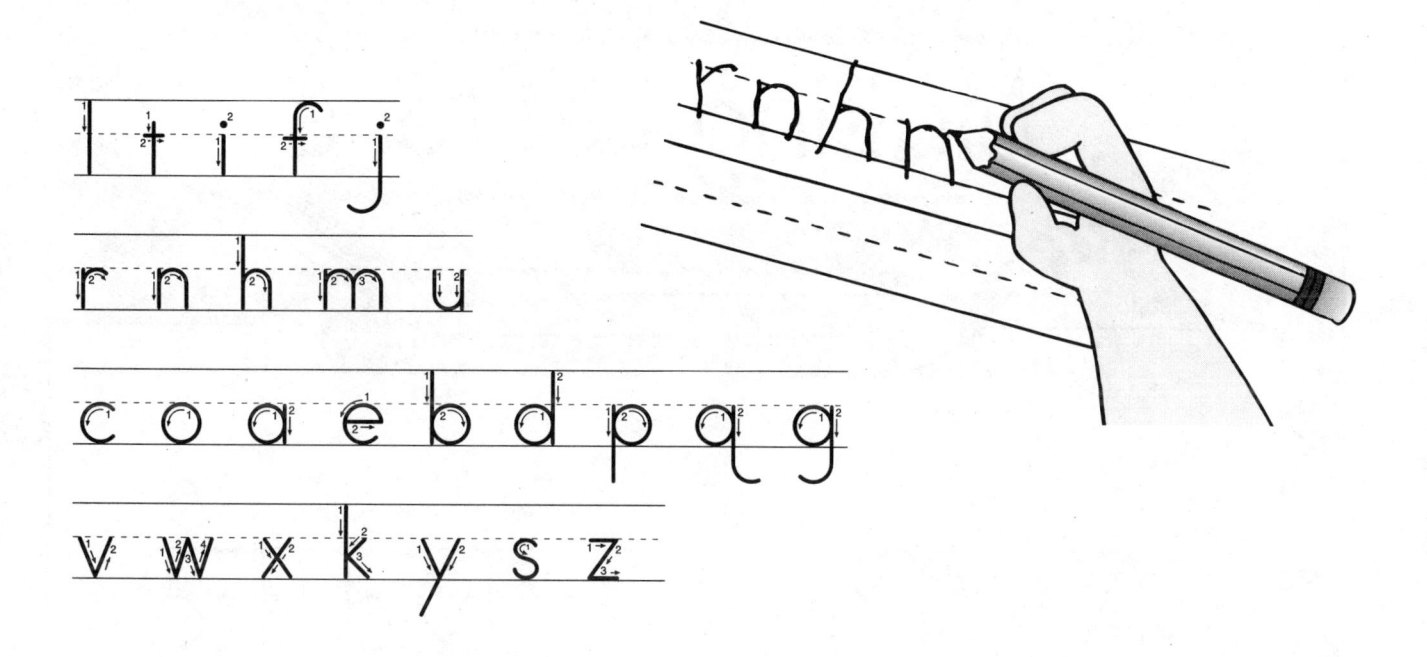

t i f j

r n h m u

c o a e b d p q g

v w x k y s z

Tips for Teaching Printing

Kindergarten children can print on unlined paper or be provided with large, faint lines that can act as guidelines for their work if they choose to recognize these lines.

Lined paper should be introduced to children in grade one.

Consistency in notebook lines is important for children in grades one and two. Teach children to bring letters up and down to specific positions on the form of lined paper you will be using. Confer with other teachers so consistency will be carried into the next grade.

I have a goldfish. It is orange and yellow.

Creative writing is not a printing lesson.
Make separate times for printing and story writing.

This desk-top print reminder will be photocopied and laminated.

Making Letters

Aa Bb Cc Dd Ee
Ff Gg Hh Ii Jj Kk
Ll Mm Nn Oo Pp
Qq Rr Ss Tt Uu
Vv Ww Xx Yy Zz

Uppercase Alphabet

Photocopy the letters on the next six pages. Cut out the letters and enlarge to the desired size. Laminate. The letters are now ready for use in a number of games found in this book.

A	B	C
D	E	F
G	H	I
J	K	

L	M	N
O	P	Q
R	S	T
U	V	W
X	Y	Z

Lowercase Alphabet

a	b	c
d	e	f
g	h	i
j	k	a

l	m	n
o	p	q
r	s	t
u	v	w
x	y	z

Upper/Lowercase Alphabet

Aa	Bb	Cc
Dd	Ee	Ff
Gg	Hh	Ii
Jj	Kk	Bb

Ll	Mm	Nn
Oo	Pp	Qq
Rr	Ss	Tt
Uu	Vv	Ww
Xx	Yy	Zz

Chapter 2

Sounds, Sounds, They're All Around!

Oral Language Experience

Oral language experience is very important for language development, particularly in the child's first years of language acquisition. Children must learn how to make sense of oral communications before they can fully understand the written language. Educational research has demonstrated that language development progress depends upon an integration of oral, reading and writing skill development. Recent research even indicates that auditory discrimination and refinements in speech play a role in the effectiveness of a child's ability to make sense of print.

Oral communication is a combination of speaking and listening, both of which will play a key role in a child's success as he gains an understanding of the world of print. Given the opportunities, children will use oral language to communicate needs, ideas, feelings and information as well as for play, song and the sheer joy of hearing the sound of their own voice!

Provide many opportunities for children to observe, mimic and experiment with new sounds and words. Oral language experience can take place in one-on-one language experiences with peers, volunteers, school staff, or the educator and in front of larger audiences in casual or formal settings.

The oral component of your language program should be central to all tasks. Oral language skills will translate to confidence and competence in all areas of language development. You may be surprised to find out that children in a safe learning environment will love to share their thoughts and written works.

Let's Listen!

Offer a variety of oral language experiences and reinforce listening skills with these simple listening games.

Listen and Move

With a little space for movement and a CD or cassette player, you can engage children in an active listening activity.

Have children find their own space and prepare to listen for the music. When the music plays, the children move. When the music stops, the children freeze.

Listen and Tell

Provide opportunities for children to tell and/or listen to stories on a daily basis. These stories can be oral tales, read-aloud stories, shared book experience or experience chart sessions.

Create a quiet atmosphere free from distractions that will make active listening possible. Allow for discussion of the reading material. Encourage thought about the story. How well are children listening?

Listen to a Storyteller

Invite a professional storyteller or learn some tips of the trade to enhance your own storytelling skills. Engaging children in a story without visual aids will help to develop listening skills and attention span.

Sharing Time

Children will develop listening and speaking skills with this twist on show-and-tell. Set aside time each day for children to share something special with the group: an object, a story or an exciting bit of news or information. In addition to a routine sharing time, provide opportunities for spontaneous sharing throughout the day.

What Would Happen If . . . ?

Materials

- ✓ cassette player and tape
- ✓ "start" and "stop" labels for cassette buttons
- ✓ printed situations

Get Ready

1. Prepare a cassette player with labeled "start" and "stop" buttons.
2. Prepare What if . . . cards to be placed at the center.
3. Consider these examples:
   What if . . .
   > the clouds were made of gelatin?
   > the ground were a trampoline?
   > animals could talk?
   > there were no school?

What to Do

1. Teach the children how to start and stop recording on the cassette player.
2. Read the What if . . . scenario of the day. Have children press the start button, offer their response to the scenario and then press the stop button.
3. Play the responses back to the group at the end of the day. The children will enjoy hearing their thoughts as well as those of their friends.

Listen for the Letter

Engage young learners with this simple captivating game that reinforces sound recognition and develops listening skills.

Get Ready

1. Have children listen very carefully to the letter sound of the day.
2. Have children repeat the sound in a giant voice, a tiny voice, a squeaky voice, a whispery voice, a gruff voice and so on.
3. Have children suggest words that contain the letter sound. Write these on chart paper or the chalkboard. Invite them to come up and circle the letter sound in the word.
4. Prior to the day, choose poems, songs or stories that contain many examples of this letter sound and print them on an "experience" chart.

How to Play

1. Read or sing together one of the poems you have written on the experience chart.
2. Have children help you circle all of the examples of the letter sound.
3. Now read it over again asking children to do one of the following when they hear the day's letter sound: raise their hand, raise a finger, raise an elbow, raise a foot, smile, clap, snap, stomp, silent cheer.
4. Encourage students to follow along as you read the chart together.
5. Action, visual clues and auditory clues will help children connect the letter to the sound and allow for some zany, active letter learning fun.

Try This

✓ Go around the circle inviting the group to say each child's name when you point to the child. Ask the children to nod their heads "yes" if they hear the letter sound of the day in the name.

Leaping Letters

A sound recognition game to keep young learners active!

Materials

- ✓ chart paper
- ✓ colored markers

Get Ready

1. Help children to master particular letter sounds.
2. Choose a poem, song or story that features the newly mastered letter.
3. Write the selection on the paper.

What to Do

1. Share a poem, story or song using an experience chart. Have children listen for the sound as you read the chart together.
2. Have children come to the front and circle the letter sound with a marker.
3. Now, have some active fun! Read the selection as a group.
4. Have children spread out and squat, ready to read together.
5. When children hear the sound they can leap to their feet like a frog and then squat down again.

Letter Links

In this letter and word association game, children further their letter recognition and auditory discrimination skills and improve their ability to identify and use nouns and adjectives.

Materials

✓ one set of laminated alphabet cards

How to Play

1. Have children sit in a circle around you.
2. Present the letter cards to the children in a fan facedown.
3. Ask one child to pull a letter card and name the letter on the card.
4. Ask the child to call out the first word that he thinks of that begins with the letter on the card.
5. This child is now the leader. Children are asked to raise their hands when they think of a word that begins with the letter on the card. The leader calls upon one child at a time until there are no more raised hands.
6. Replace the letter card in the deck, and ask another child to pull a card.
7. Play continues as before.

Try This

✓ Have the leader choose a noun as his word. Ask the other children to describe the person, place or thing named by the leader using words that start with the letter on the card.
✓ Ask the child who draws the card to think of as many words as she can that begin with the letter. Then replace the card and have a different child choose a card.

Broken Telephone

Materials

- ✓ circle of children
- ✓ good listening ears!

How to Play

1. Sit on the floor with the children sitting around you in a circle.
2. Think of a message and whisper it in the ear of the child to your left.
3. That child then passes on your message—as best she can—by whispering whatever she has heard or can remember into the ear of the child on her left.
4. Play continues in this manner until the person on your right—the last person in the broken telephone line—receives the message. He must then repeat aloud the message he has received.
5. The original messenger—you, in this case—then reveals the original message.
6. Choose a different messenger and play again.

Alliteration Name Game

*Kids love alliteration, and books for young children—especially alphabet books—
are **f**ull of **ph**rases that **feature** these **f**anciful and **f**unctional **f**orm.
By using their own names (words with which kids are intimately acquainted)
as a platform for learning, kids feel secure enough to experiment with language.
And by searching for good, and bad, descriptors for themselves,
children have fun with words while learning a little bit about proper nouns and adjectives.*

Angry Annie, Beautiful Benjamin, Caring Caitlyn, Daring David, Energetic Elizabeth, Frightened Frank, Gracious Grace, Hilarious Henry, Intriguing Isabella, Joking Jamal, Kindly Katie, Laughing Larry, Marvelous Maria, Nibbling Nathan, Obvious Orrin, Pretty Paige, Quiet Quinn, Radical Rosa, Silly Samuel, Tricky Tracey, Upside-down Ulysses, Vibrant Valerie, Wacky Walter, X-ray Xaviera, Yodeling Yves and Zany Zelda

Materials

- ✓ chalkboard or flip chart
- ✓ chalk or markers
- ✓ paper

Kindly Katie

What to Do

1. To get the ball rolling, print your first name on the chalkboard or a flip chart. Have the children brainstorm adjectives in a circle or at their desks. (Despite the "letter perfectness" of the example above, alliteration is about the sound, not spelling. *Gentle* is fine with *Jenny*, but does not work with *Grant*.)
2. Write all of the suggestions on the board or chart.
3. Try different combinations with your name. As a group, decide which words best describe you. Which words don't fit at all? Which are the nicest? Which are the silliest?
4. Write down all successful combinations.
5. Make a Big, Boastful, Brag Book. On the cover, have the child print his favorite descriptive alliteration word before his name and draw a picture to illustrate the adjective. Inside the booklet, use each page to "show and tell" a different combination: Angry Annie, Artistic Annie, Angelic Annie, Argumentative Annie and Awesome Annie.

Author's Note: *Some children–those with names that begin with Q, U, X and Z, for example–are going to be more difficult to describe. Use the challenge to an advantage by taking the opportunity to introduce the children to the dictionary. For little Zachary, browse the "Z" pages reading appropriate words out loud until one of them catches his fancy or tickles his funny bone. Define the word in a way that Zachary can understand, and let him decide whether or not it suits his personality. Start a list and add to it a number of "Zany Zack" words.*

Try This

- ✓ Brainstorm in small groups or one large circle to develop an adjective list for each child in the class. Make individual lists for each child.

Musical Associations

In this musical activity that improves creative and abstract thinking, children learn that language is inspired by the world around them.

Materials

- ✓ CD, cassette or record player
- ✓ variety of musical selections representing different musical styles (jazz, blues, rock, country, classical, opera, etc.)
- ✓ chalkboard or flip chart
- ✓ chalk or marker

What to Do

1. Play a short musical piece.
2. When the music stops, have the children shout out how the music makes them feel or what it makes them think about. There are no limits. They can express an emotion–happy, sad, angry–or an action–jumping up and down, running in circles, sleeping–or an event–riding a horse, playing hockey, eating dinner. The object is to allow the music to speak to a child and for the child to find words to describe what the music has said.
3. Write all the responses on the board.
4. Ask the children to make up a name for the piece of music.
5. Write all the titles on the board.
6. Make up a concert program using the names of pieces and the thoughts or feelings they inspire.
7. Send home copies of the concert program, or distribute them to another class. Host the concert in your classroom. Have the children act out a musical drama to each piece. *(This can be an ad lib performance–it doesn't have to be choreographed. Just make sure the kids' actions are in accordance with the song descriptions.)*

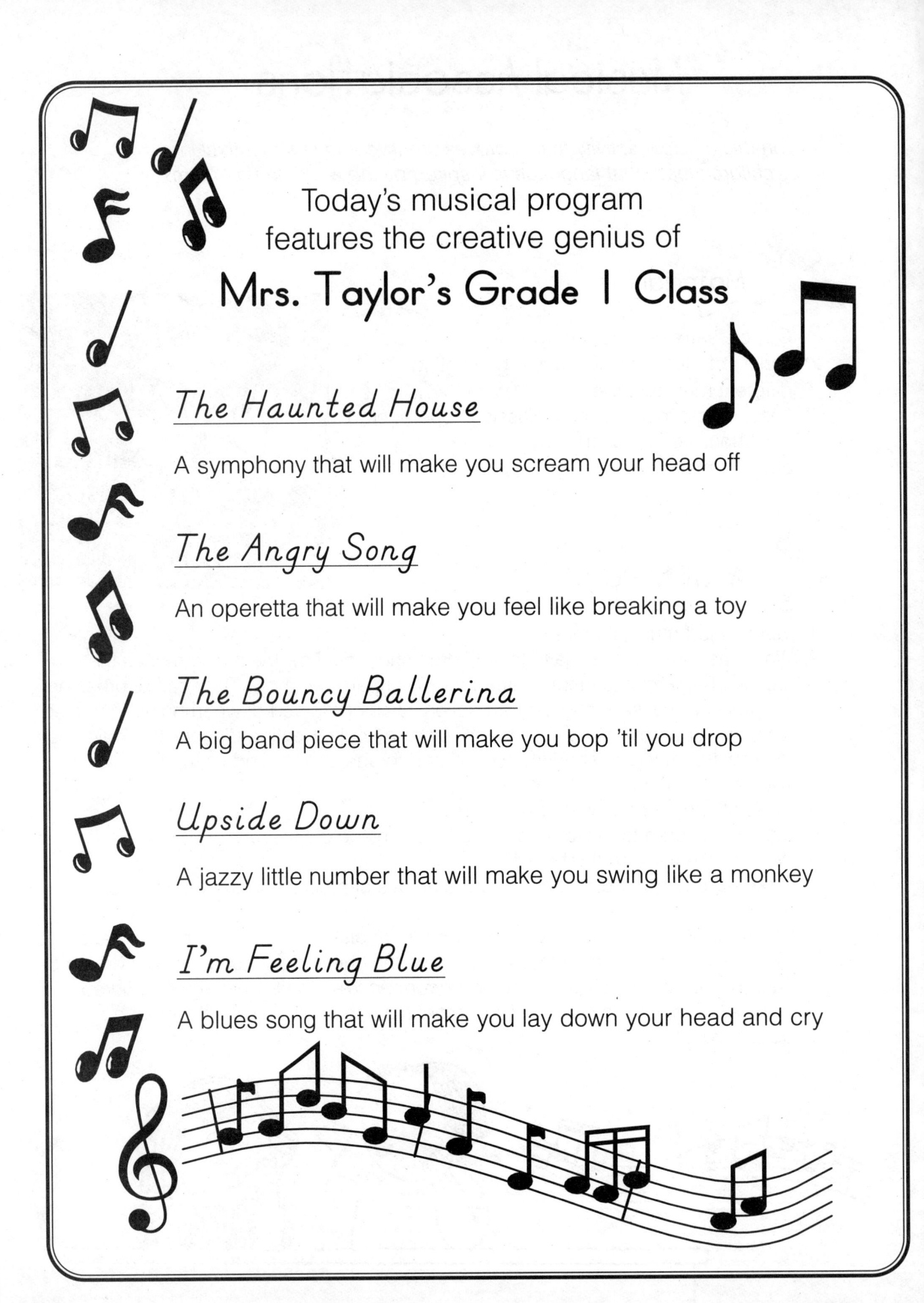

Today's musical program
features the creative genius of
Mrs. Taylor's Grade 1 Class

The Haunted House
A symphony that will make you scream your head off

The Angry Song
An operetta that will make you feel like breaking a toy

The Bouncy Ballerina
A big band piece that will make you bop 'til you drop

Upside Down
A jazzy little number that will make you swing like a monkey

I'm Feeling Blue
A blues song that will make you lay down your head and cry

Clowning Around with Language

By looking at the silly side of language to expand vocabulary and enhance printing skills, children learn that words can be funny and writing can be fun!

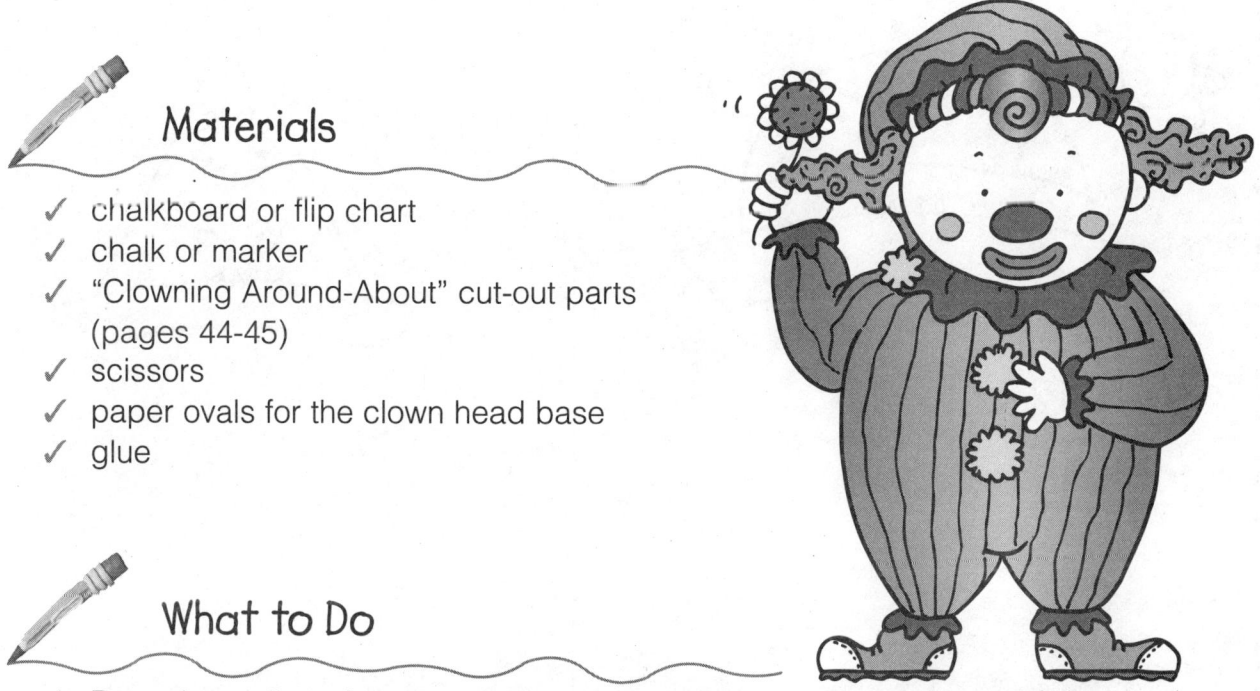

Materials

- ✓ chalkboard or flip chart
- ✓ chalk or marker
- ✓ "Clowning Around-About" cut-out parts (pages 44-45)
- ✓ scissors
- ✓ paper ovals for the clown head base
- ✓ glue

What to Do

1. Draw the outline of a clown face on the board.
2. Talk about what kind of things make kids laugh and what words they use when they want to sound funny.
3. Brainstorm to come up with the world's silliest words. They can be "real" words or entirely new constructions. They just have to sound funny.
4. Write each word on the board or chart.
5. When the list is complete, have each child choose one word as the name for his Clowning Around-About (*Oopsy-Daisy* the Clown, *Wacky* the Clown, *La La* the Clown, *Toot-Toot* the Clown, *Speeny* the Clown, etc.)
6. Back at their desks, have the children cut out, assemble and paste together their Clowning Around-Abouts, printing the name of their silly word on the clown's hat in the black provided.
7. Hang the clowns around the classroom as a reminder that language doesn't *have* to be dull and writing doesn't *have* to be serious.

43

Clowning Around-Abouts Cut-Outs

_____
the clown

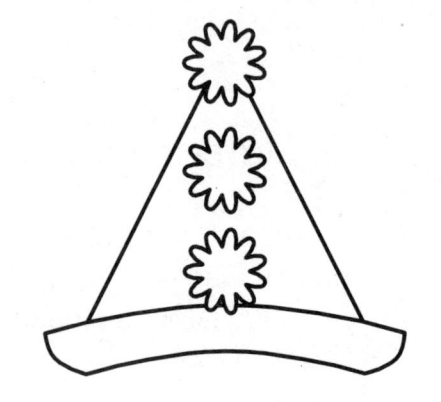

_____
the clown

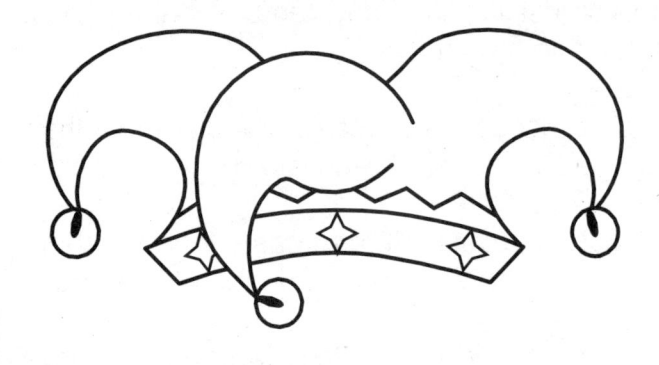

_____
the clown

_____
the clown

44

Clowning Around-Abouts Cut-Outs

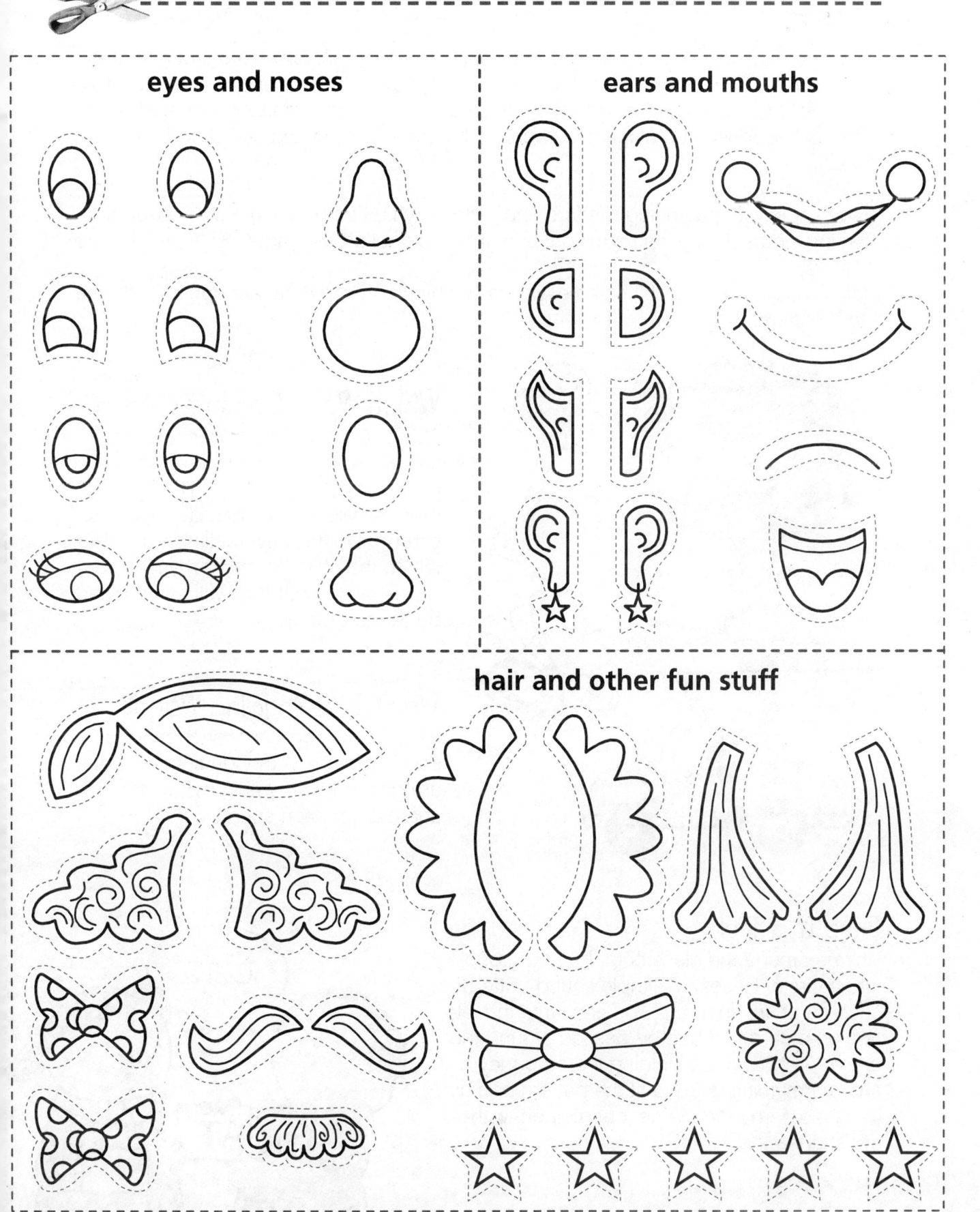

eyes and noses

ears and mouths

hair and other fun stuff

45

Poetry Power

Poetry sets the stage for wonderful word play. It opens children's ears and hearts to the wonderful sounds and meanings of words and provides a steppingstone to reading experience. Learning about rhyming words will give children tools to help them read, look for cues and clues and share in the experience of patterned and predictable books.

Start simple with beginning readers and writers by first introducing the concept of rhyming words. Focus on rhyming words that are spelled the same.

Words that rhyme sound the same. Focus on rhyming words that are spelled with the same pattern.

Which Word Doesn't Belong?
Play a listening game. Recite a list of four words, three of which share simple rhyme and one that doesn't. Have children tell you which word doesn't belong. Do this several times and then talk to the children about rhyming words–a concept they will have already begun to grasp!

What Is a Rhyming Word?
Explain that rhyming words share a sound pattern. Although some sounds are different in rhyming words, they share a common sound.

Give It a Try!
Rhyme around the classroom. Put the group into a circle. Choose a simple sound pattern such as *at, in, an* and *it*. You can write the letters on a card that can be passed around the circle. A child who is holding the card may share a rhyming word to fit the pattern or may pass the card onto the next participant without sharing.

What Is a Poem?

Poems are pieces of writing that usually follow a pattern of rhythm and rhyme. Poems are made up of ideas, syllables, rhyming words and patterns. They sometimes tell a little story or tell us something about a person, place, thing or feeling. In a poem, the way the words sound is often as important as what they mean, so listen carefully!

Share a Poem

Bring the wonder of poetry to children by sharing some of your favorite poems.

Memorize and recite a poem. This will help draw children into the oral language experience of a poem. What did they notice about the reading?

Let's Take a Look

Share a poem using an experience chart, overhead or other visual aid. Have children listen for the rhyming words and help mark these on your visual aid. This exercise will give children a sound context for development of a sight vocabulary and will open doors to early reading experiences.

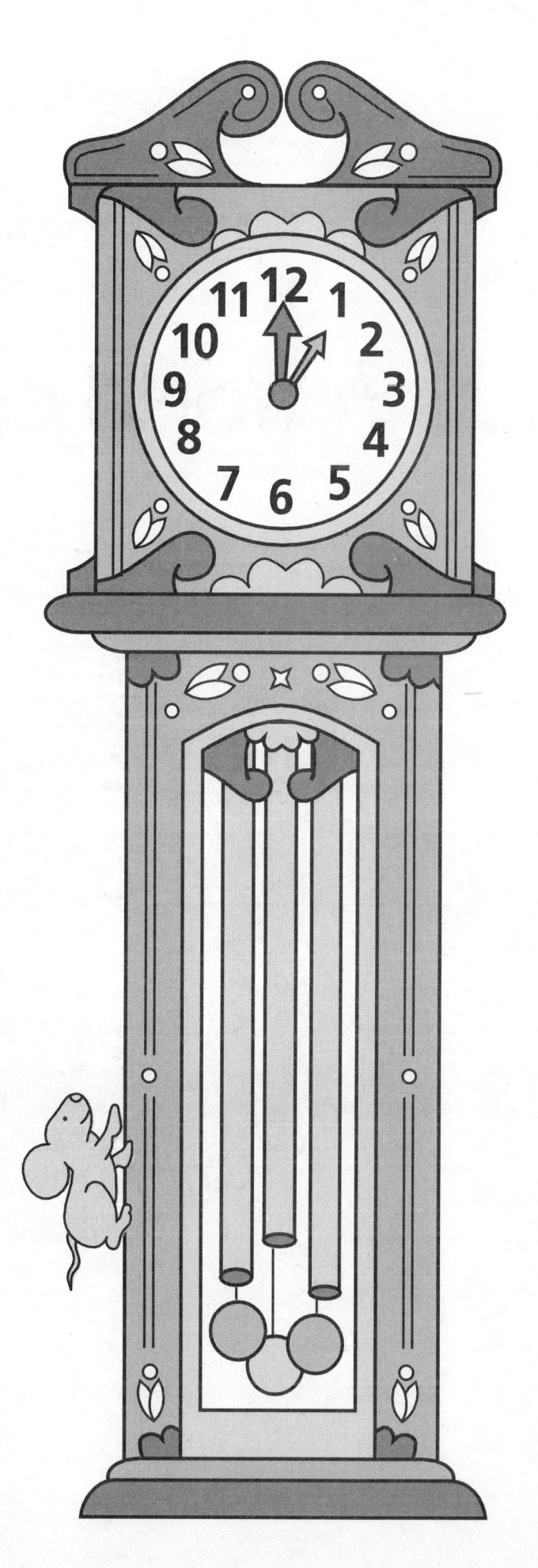

Chapter 3

A World of Words

Pick a Card

This activity promotes letter recognition and proper pronunciation, enhances vocabulary and reinforces the concept of taking turns.

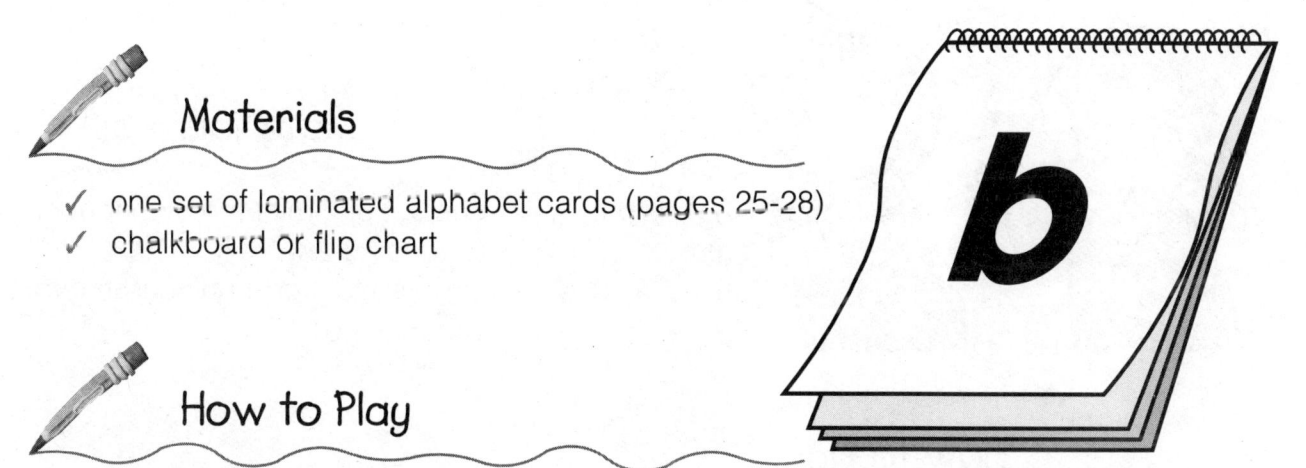

Materials

- ✓ one set of laminated alphabet cards (pages 25-28)
- ✓ chalkboard or flip chart

How to Play

1. Have children sit in a circle.
2. Ask one child to pick a card and say out loud the name of the letter on the card.
3. Write the letter at the top of the board or chart.
4. Ask the child to think of a word that begins with the letter on the card.
5. Write the word on the board or chart.
6. Ask the children to raise their hands if they know a word that starts with the letter on the card.
7. Add these words to the list.
8. Have the children "read" the complete list.
9. Point to individual words and have children raise their hands to "read" them.
10. Have the child replace the letter and repeat the process if desired.
11. Keep the letter lists for use in an alphabet book. (See page 54.)

Try This

- ✓ Lay out the alphabet cards in the middle of the circle (either randomly or in alphabetical order). Make the sound of a letter. Ask the children to raise their hand if they know the letter that makes that sound. Have a child pick the letter from the middle of the circle. The game continues as above.

Word Tag

Letter recognition, vocabulary expansion and turn taking are the natural outcomes of this game, which is a variation of conventional children's tag.

Materials

- one set of laminated alphabet cards (pages 25-28)
- large space for running (the gym or school yard)

How to Play

1. Show the children the laminated alphabet cards and have them identify each letter and its sound.
2. Choose one child to be "it."
3. He must think of a word that begins with the letter on the card.
4. The other children begin running as soon as the child who is "it" says his word out loud.
5. When another child is tagged, she must think of a new word that begins with the letter on the card.
6. Play continues as above.

Try This

- Play this game in the classroom, with children seated at their desks. The person who is "it" leaves her seat and taps another person on the shoulder. The first "it" returns to her desk. The new "it" must think of a new word that begins with the letter on the card. Play continues as above.

- Try this game in a circle as with the Duck, Duck, Goose game. The first "goose" is asked to think of a word that begins with the letter on the card and walks around the perimeter of the circle tapping the "ducks" gently on the head or shoulder as he repeats the word. When he gets to the next "goose," he will say a different word that begins with the letter on the card. The new "goose" jumps to her feet and races the first goose back to her spot in the circle. The person who is still standing is the new "goose." She repeats the new word and play continues as above.

Alphabet Excursions

This activity reinforces letter recognition, alphabetical sequencing, theme appropriateness and turn taking and introduces the concept of consensus building.

I went to the zoo, and I saw an aardvark.
I went to the zoo, and I saw an aardvark *and a baboon.*
I went to the zoo, and I saw an aardvark, a baboon *and a cheetah.*
I went to the zoo, and I saw an aardvark, a baboon, a cheetah *and a donkey.*
I went to the zoo, and I saw an aardvark, a baboon, a cheetah, a donkey *and . . .*

Materials

- ✓ one set of laminated alphabet cards (pages 25-28)
- ✓ strips of paper and marker (optional)
- ✓ "Alphabet Excursion" ideas: I went to the store and I bought . . .
  I wrote a letter to Santa and I asked for . . .
  I went to a restaurant and I ordered . . .
  I went on a camping trip and I took . . .
  I went on a vacation and I saw . . .

How to Play

1. Have children sit in a circle around you.
2. You will go first. Hold up the letter "A" card and make your excursion statement: "I went to the zoo, and I saw an . . . aardvark." Your turn is now over.
3. Hold up the "B" card. The child to your left must then think of a noun (in this case an animal) that begins with the letter "B." When he has made his excursion statement: "I went to the zoo, and I saw a . . . baboon," his turn is over.
4. Play continues until the class has wandered all the way through the alphabet.
5. Encourage the children to use their imaginations. If a child can't think of a word, brainstorm as a group or have her make one up. (For the letter "X," the child might see a "Xanther" or a "Xantelope" or even a "Xassinoose.") The sentences can be as sensible–or as silly–as the children want them to be!

Try This

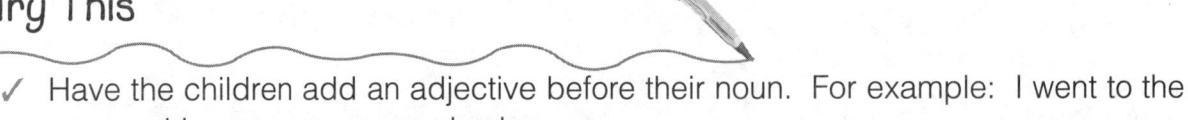

- ✓ Have the children add an adjective before their noun. For example: I went to the zoo, and I saw an *angry* aardvark.
- ✓ Write out each sentence on a slip of paper. When your excursion is over, string these sentences together in alphabetical order and hang in the classroom. The strings can be repeated daily for reinforcement of the alphabet concept.

Angry Aardvark

Happy Hippo

Bashful Bear

Pass the Package

Letter recognition, alphabetical sequencing, thematic concepts, turn taking and consensus building.

Materials

- ✓ one set of laminated alphabet cards (pages 25-28)
- ✓ one set of magnetic letters (or other three-dimensional alphabet set)
- ✓ tissue paper
- ✓ two markers
- ✓ tape

How to Play

1. Have children sit in a circle.
2. Hold up a laminated alphabet card. Ask someone to tell you the name of the letter and to find the matching magnetic letter.
3. Wrap the letter loosely in a thin layer of tissue paper and tape in place.
4. Have another child choose a word that starts with the letter. Write this word on the tissue paper, using one marker for the first letter and another marker for the other letters.
5. Have children pass the package around the circle as they sing the "The Word on the Package" sung to the tune of "The Wheels on the Bus."
   The word on the package is "alphabet," "alphabet," "alphabet."
   The word on the package is "alphabet," and it begins with "A."
6. When the song stops, whoever is holding the package must think of another word that starts with that letter.
7. Wrap another layer of tissue paper around the package. Tape loosely and write the new word on the package. Sing the song substituting the new word.

Try This

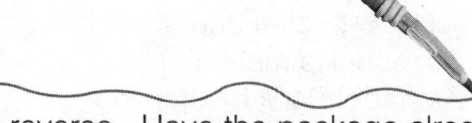

- ✓ Play the game in reverse. Have the package already wrapped in layers with different words written on each layer. At the end of each round, the child holding the package unwraps one layer and must try to read the word that is uncovered. Play continues until the letter is unwrapped.

Alphabooks

By combining audio, visual and tactile elements, this activity helps to promote recognition of the shape and sound of each letter of the alphabet.

Materials

- ✓ one enlarged alphabet set (pages 25-30)
- ✓ glue
- ✓ stapler
- ✓ sprinkle material (glitter, confetti, rice, popcorn kernels, tissue paper, etc.)
- ✓ container
- ✓ scissors (optional)

What to Do

1. Make a booklet using one letter of the enlarged alphabet set as the cover page.
2. Have the children trace the letter on the cover of the booklet with glue and sprinkle with the sprinkle material.
3. Shake off the excess sprinkle material into a container.
4. Use the letter list from Pick a Card game (page 49) or make a new list of words that start with the letter on the cover of the book. Put one of these words on each page of the booklet.
5. Have the children draw and color a picture to illustrate each word.

Try This

- ✓ Cut the pages of the booklet in the shape of the letter so that the finished product is a *Letter Shape Book*.
- ✓ Have the child trace the first letter of the word on each page of the booklet with glue and sprinkle with glitter (or other flat sprinkle material.)
- ✓ Create a *Complete Alphabet Book* by stapling together the 26 cover pages. Use glue and a flat sprinkle material to decorate each page. (Children could draw and color pictures that correspond to words on the letter list on each letter page.)

Signs, Symbols, Labels and Logos

By kindergarten most children are capable of recognizing and taking meaning from some amount of print. The children may not even recognize their "reading ability" until you point it out.

Get Ready

Compile a file with samples of popular symbols and logos, i.e. the symbols for restrooms, the logos for popular sports teams, automobiles, food chains, cereal boxes, candy wrappers, directional arrows, open and closed signs, a "no dogs allowed" sign and so on.

What to Do

1. Display well-known signs, symbols and logos for your class.
2. Find out who knows what the various samples mean or represent.
3. Show enthusiasm for the children's ability to recognize and read signs and labels.

Try This

- ✓ Invite children and their parents to go on a hunt for familiar symbols and labels that can be copied, drawn or brought into the classroom.
- ✓ Who can recognize the various samples?
- ✓ You and the children can compile the samples into an *I Can Read* scrapbook that can be referenced throughout the year by eager new readers.

Dear Parent/Guardian,

At school today the children were very excited to find out that they could read!

The children discovered that they could read many of the signs, symbols, labels and logos that they find around their homes, school and community every day.

Young children are learning to recognize that meaning is attributed to various symbols and letters. This is an important step towards making sense of print.

You can help your child gain confidence in their ability to make sense of print by discovering signs, symbols, labels and logos together. Can your child distinguish between a can of soup and a can of tomatoes by looking at the label? Can your child recognize a favorite team logo? If you let your child know how proud you are of his "reading" ability, he will gain confidence and be enthusiastic about learning more about reading and writing when he is ready.

We are making an *I Can Read* scrapbook in class to collect these signs, symbols, labels and logos for reference. We would appreciate any contributions to this class project.

Thank you for your participation.

Sincerely,

The Sorting Game

Put signs and labels to good use in this simple sorting game.

Materials

- clothes basket
- two or more hoops, depending upon level of difficulty of game
- sturdy signs and labels
- props for the sorting game:
    - boots, mittens and hats
    - red, green and white items
    - large, medium and small blocks, beads, toys or books
    - Christmas cards, Valentine's Day cards and birthday cards
    - letters printed on cards (combination of three letters)
    - upper- and lowercase letters printed on cards
    - numbers and letters

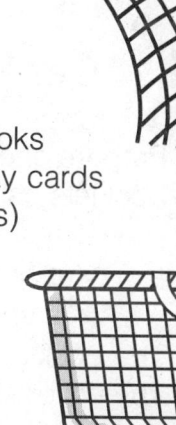

What to Do

1. Set the hoops about 6" (15 cm) apart from one another and about 12" (30 cm) from the basket of props.
2. Instruct children to put one sign or label in front of each hoop.
3. Have children sort the prop items one at a time into the proper hoop.
4. This can be done as a group by selecting one child at a time to take an item to the labeled hoop while the others look on, or as an individual activity during free choice activity time. When an individual has sorted all of the items, the educator and/or group of peers can be asked to check for accuracy.

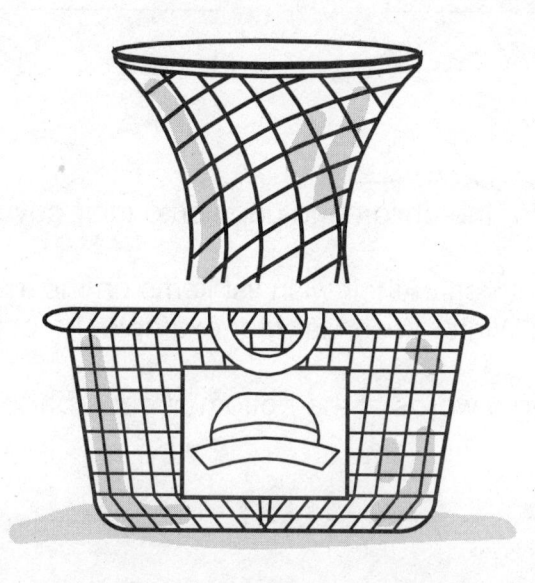

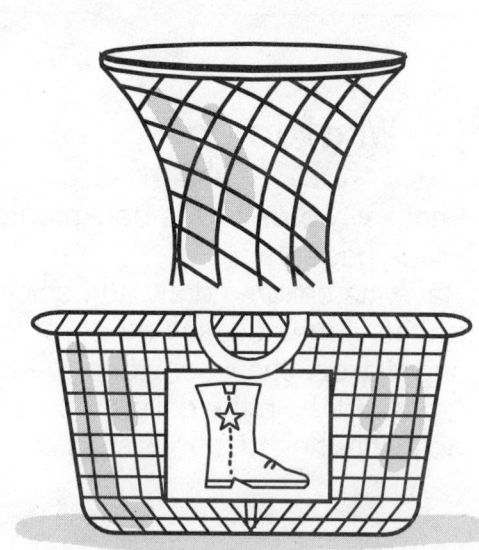

Wish Lists

In this activity, children use picture symbols to communicate.

Materials

✓ *Wish List* booklets (one for each child)
✓ crayons or markers

Get Ready

1. Prepare one *Wish List* booklet for each child. The *Wish List* booklets can celebrate:
    ✓ a season (My Winter Wish List/My Summer Wish List)
    ✓ a holiday (My Christmas Wish List/My Hanukkah Wish List)
    ✓ a special event (My Birthday Wish List)

   The booklet should have a cover and several inside pages.

2. The cover should look like this:

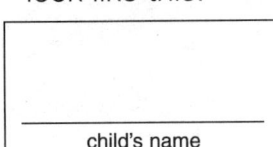

   _____
   child's name

   _____
   name of event/
   celebration/season

   Wish List

3. The first inside page should read:

   This
   _____
   name of event/
   celebration

   I would like . . .

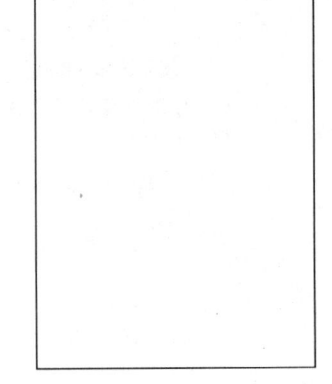

4. The other pages should be left blank.

What to Do

1. Print key words on the background for the children to copy onto their covers and inside pages.
2. Have the children draw and color pictures of their wish list items on the inside pages of their books. (For "Patrick's Winter Wish List," for example, he could draw snowflakes, snowmen, toboggans, etc.)
3. If desired, help the children print single words at the bottom of each page to describe their picture wishes.

Create a Recipe

Materials

- ✓ paper
- ✓ list of possible ingredients
- ✓ magazines for cut and paste
- ✓ writing tools

What to Do

1. Have children visit Imagination Station and read the recipe request together. Consider the following options:

    Create a recipe for . . .
    - birthday cake
    - witches' brew
    - Mom's Christmas cookies
    - Dad's meat loaf
    - harvest soup
    - dog food
    - a good friend

    Cereal Shake
    Ingredients
    - 2 scoops of your favorite ice cream
    - ½ cup skim milk
    - 2 tablespoons chocolate syrup
    - ½ cup of your favorite cereal

    Directions: Put your 2 scoops of ice cream in a blender (have an adult help you with this part). Then add the skim milk and chocolate syrup. Blend til smooth. Pour into a glass and stir in your favorite treat. Enjoy!

2. Have children create recipes. They can write the recipes or draw the ingredients and directions. The recipe reference card will assist beginning writers.

Create a Recipe

Ingredients

eggs	peanut butter	mud
milk	sugar	sand
water	salt	meatballs
flour	chocolate chips	flies
bowl	spoon	pour
add	mix	bake

Emotion Promotion

In this happy/sad face cut-out activity, children learn how to put their feelings into words and learn a little about adjectives in the process.

Materials

- Happy Face/Sad Face Cut-Outs (page 62)
- chalkboard or flip chart
- chalk or marker
- scissors
- pencils
- glue (optional)
- wooden craft sticks or straws and modeling clay (optional)

What to Do

1. Photocopy, cut and enlarge the happy and sad faces on page 62.
2. Draw a happy face on the board (or chart).
3. Ask the children to think of words that describe how it feels to be happy.
4. Draw a sad face on the board (or chart).
5. Ask the children to think of words that describe how it feels to be sad.
6. Fill each face with descriptive words.
7. Hand out the happy face/sad face cut-outs. Have the children copy their favorite happy and sad words on the correct faces.

Try This

- Play the Opposite Game. Use the two faces simultaneously. You choose a descriptive word–smile, for example–and print it on the appropriate face. The children must think of the opposite. You then print the opposite on the other face. Have the children put the opposites on the happy/sad face cut-outs. Glue the two faces together with a craft stick or straw in between. Press the stick into a ball of modeling clay. Children can use the happy face/sad face "puppet" as a mood indicator on their desks or at home.

Happy Face/Sad Face Cut-Outs

Sensational Seasons

In this activity, children learn how to discriminate between the seasons, and to categorize their observations using appropriate nouns, adjectives and graphical representations.

Materials

- ✓ Sensational Seasons Cut-Outs (page 64)
- ✓ chalkboard or flip chart
- ✓ chalk or marker
- ✓ colored paper: white, blue, yellow, orange and white
- ✓ colored pencils or markers
- ✓ glue
- ✓ string

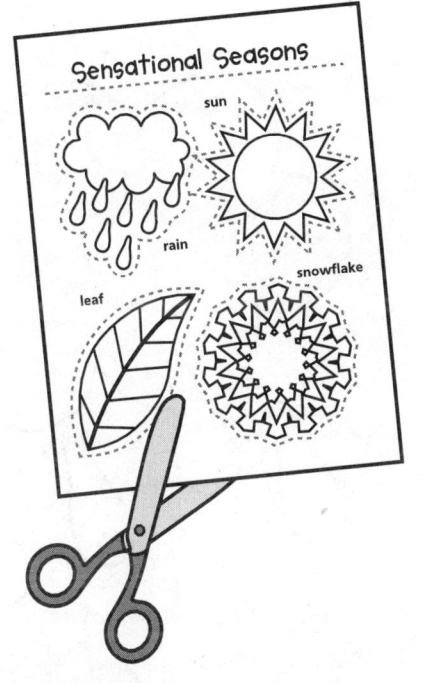

What to Do

1. Depending on the season, prepare one of the Sensational Seasons cut-outs. (spring–raindrops, summer–sun, autumn–leaf, winter–snowflake)
2. Have the children gather around the chalkboard (or chart).
3. Reproduce the season shape on the board or (chart).
4. Brainstorm to develop a list of words that represent the season.
5. Print these inside the seasonal shape.
6. Back at their desks, have children copy the descriptive words from the board onto their seasonal cut-outs using pencil crayon (if they are comfortable without the capacity to erase mistakes). They should use both cut-outs, printing different words on each.
7. Have the children place one of their cut-outs facedown on the desk. Coat with glue. Lay the end of the string in the glue. Place the other cut-out, face-up, on top of the glue and string. Press and hold in place. (Make sure the two cut-outs are arranged so that the words will be oriented when the cut-out spins around on its string.)
8. Suspend the cut-outs from the ceiling.

LC10201 Copyright © Teaching & Learning Company, Carthage, IL 62321-0010

Sensational Seasons Cut-Outs

sun

rain

snowflake

leaf

Learning to Spell

Spelling is important for communicating through print. Children in these early grades are mastering an awareness of print, letter names, letter sounds and making use of this exciting new code as they decipher reading material and construct their own works of writing. Spelling is a complicated skill that is mastered in stages.

How Can I Teach Spelling?

The spelling program should provide a variety of approaches to spelling instruction: specific formal lessons and tasks, opportunities for spelling experimentation and discovery through play, and opportunities for spelling practice and imitation through the establishment of a rich language environment.

Children develop an awareness of and efficiency in spelling in their own individual ways. An effective, ongoing evaluation program will provide information about the needs of each child in your class.

A spelling program should help children learn to recognize and reproduce the words they are most often exposed to and should help them to develop an awareness of spelling rules and sounds that will carry with them through their lives.

A good speller will happily engage in writing tasks, feeling confident that the skills he possesses will allow him to communicate effectively through print.

Practice Makes Perfect

The best way for children to become good spellers is through daily writing experiences that range from journal writing to word lists and weekly spelling dictation. Daily writing activities provide opportunities for children to practice their spelling skills as they develop in all areas of language arts.

Early Spelling Strategies

Group Language Experience Lessons
Group lessons involving the use of language experience charts will help reinforce letter names, letter sounds, phonetics, vowel and consonant concepts and auditory discrimination. Experience charts help improve and increase sight vocabulary that will transfer to written work.

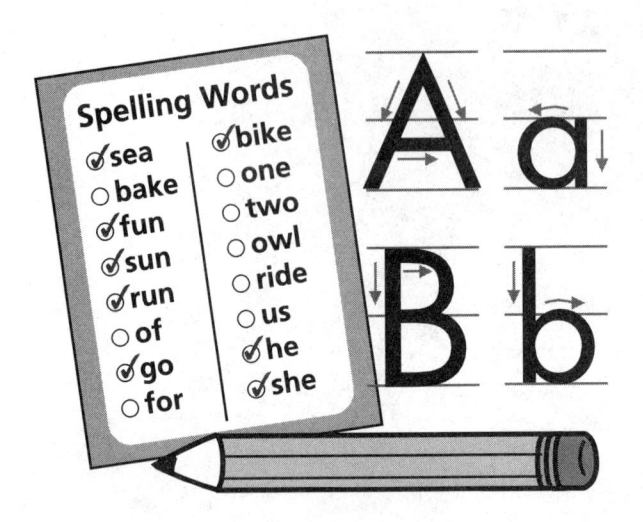

Inventive Spelling
Inventive spelling is an important step towards standard spelling. Young writers must learn to crawl before they can walk, so room must be allowed for early spelling experiences. Encourage children to experiment, practice and feel pride in their early writing attempts.

Inventive spelling is an important step on the road to standard spelling and should be recognized as a great accomplishment for children who are beginning to put sounds into print.

Standard Spelling for Early Writers
Children begin to develop a sight vocabulary from the time they start to read and write. Encourage standard spelling and provide opportunities for children to learn and model proper spelling through tools such as "word books" and simple spelling lists with weekly dictations.

Guides
Every child should have a letter formation template of the alphabet to reinforce newly acquired letter-making skills. Word lists should also be provided so children learn to spell new words properly. These words should appear in spelling lists and should be reinforced throughout the week through various reading and writing experiences.

Take-a-Try

Early spelling is encouraged with this simple, hands-on activity.

Materials

- ✓ recipe card holder
- ✓ recipe cards
- ✓ photos, magazine pictures, drawings, stickers or other visuals
- ✓ writing tools

Get Ready

1. Decorate a recipe box with letters (paint or stickers.)
2. Make a set of Take-a-Try cards.
3. Paste, draw or stick a picture of an easy-to-spell word on the blank side of the card.
4. Neatly print the word for the picture on the lined side of the card.

What to Do

1. Place the cards picture-side up in the box.
2. Have the children remove a card and try to spell the word for the item illustrated on the card.
3. After taking a try at the word, the child can flip over the card and check the accuracy of her spelling attempt. Words that have been mastered can be added to each child's *My Word Treasure Chest* or *My Word Book*.

My Word Treasure Chest

A "word box" variation, this child-made treasure chest holds the valuable word gems that children collect and will use throughout their lives.

Materials

- ✓ glitter markers
- ✓ markers
- ✓ Word Gem Cut-Outs (page 69)
- ✓ small shoe box or recipe file box
- ✓ aluminum foil (scrunched and then pressed flat)
- ✓ paste and glue sticks
- ✓ gem stickers
- ✓ colored tagboard (for gem shapes)
- ✓ glitter
- ✓ plastic gems

What to Do

1. Have children decorate their treasure chests.
2. The boxes can be covered with paste, layered with foil and left to dry.
3. Decorations (including gem cut-outs) can be added when the glue has dried.
4. When children master a new word, invite them to take a precut gem shape and neatly print the word on it.
5. Have them bring their word gems to you. (You can check the words and decorate with gem stickers.)
6. The new word "gem" can be placed in the child's treasure chest for future reference.

Try This

- ✓ For additional incentive, the educator can add a plastic gem to the child's treasure chest each time he acquires 10 new words.

Word Gem Cut-Outs

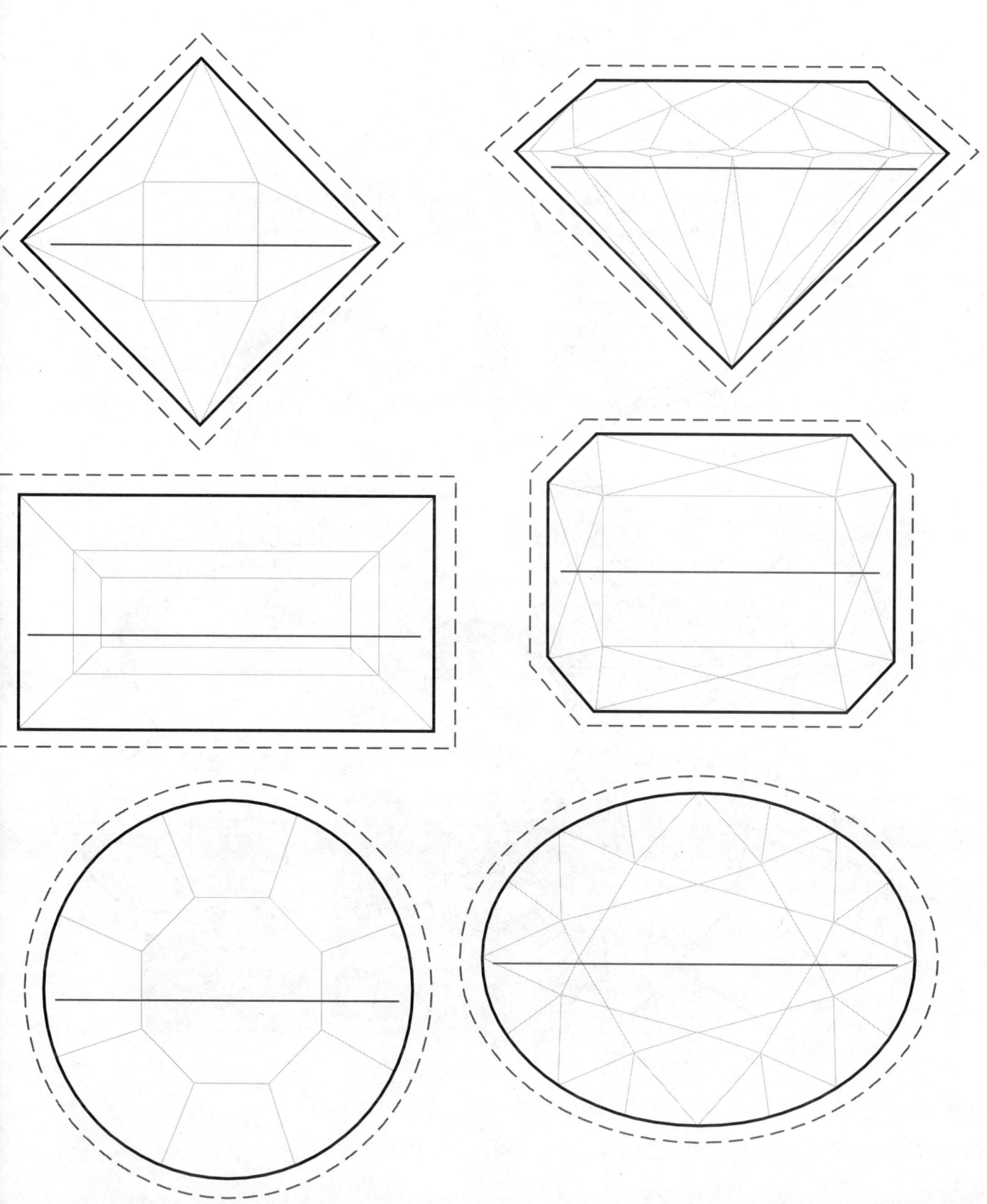

69

Chapter 4

Ready to Write

Learning to Write

Young children learn best by doing, and the best way learn to write is to practice, practice, practice. You can help children to develop writing skills and confidence by exposing them to a variety of success-oriented early writing experiences.

Young children won't be experts, but through approximations and active learning, they can take part in the wonderful process of writing. Exciting daily writing opportunities will help create competent and eager writers. If you show enthusiasm, curiosity and an interest in stories, authors and printed information, this love of writing will rub off on your students.

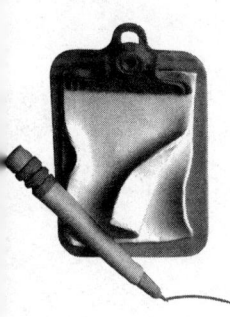

Link kids to writing with the following learning tasks and lessons:

- ✓ free exploration of letter-making materials
- ✓ formal printing lessons
- ✓ language experience chart activities
- ✓ exposure to language through poetry, song, conversation and sharing time
- ✓ access to reading, writing and role-playing center
- ✓ daily journal or story-writing activities (with approximations and drawings)
- ✓ teacher-led skill attainment lessons that are reinforced through related tasks
- ✓ exposure to new words and language
- ✓ reproductions of sight vocabulary
- ✓ the creation of a developmentally appropriate standard spelling program
- ✓ opportunities to use print for a purpose

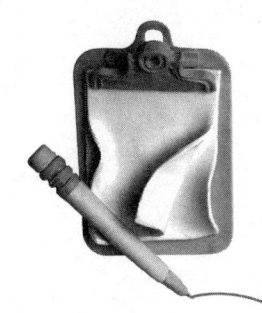

Strategies for Teaching Early Writing Skills

- ✓ Provide a space and activities that will encourage children to work independently in the company of other children.

- ✓ Encourage interaction and the sharing of ideas and work.

- ✓ Model enthusiasm for your work and the work of others.

- ✓ Get kids excited about sounds and words.

- ✓ Provide immediate oral and written responses to work as often as possible.

- ✓ Be an active partner in putting together a writing portfolio.

- ✓ Host individual student-teacher writing conferences.

- ✓ Provide oral feedback, formal assessment keys, scoring cards and grades.

- ✓ Provide group and individual review of previously taught rules and skills.

- ✓ Introduce new concepts accompanied by follow-up activities and assistance.

- ✓ Provide developmentally appropriate activities that cater to the individual.

- ✓ Integrate assessment and teaching.

- ✓ Model response and revision of your and other writers' work.

- ✓ Integrate an early writing program with reading and writing preparedness programs.

- ✓ Reinforce concepts with active tasks that allow children to explore language in a variety of interesting ways.

- ✓ Use play to help children make sense of the written world.

Kindergarten Writing Center

Children Will	Skill Development	Teacher's Role
make letters from a variety of materials	fine motor coordination letter recognition	provide stimulating letter-making materials (sand trays, chalkboards, clay)
trace letters	fine motor skills letter recognition	provide tracer letters and writing instruments (model proper pencil position)
copy letters	letter making	provide writing materials and letter models
copy words	letter making fine motor skills word and letter recognition	provide writing materials and copy words
make pictures and tell story of picture	refine fine motor skills develop storytelling skills develop sequencing skills enrich vocabulary enhance oral communication	stimulate interest through praise, participation and imitation listen attentively and ask leading questions
make books and talk about the making of a book	demonstrate an understanding of the function of print, master book-handling skills	provide story patterns encourage creative thought act as a scribe (if necessary)
ask questions	analyze one's work think about the work of another develop reading comprehension	encourage creative thought instill curiosity

Grade 1 Writing Center

Children Will	Skill Development	Teacher's Role
trace letters	refine fine motor skills letter recognition	provide writing instruments and letters to be traced
copy letters	letter making fine motor development	provide writing materials and letter models
copy words	letter making fine motor skills word and letter recognition	provide writing materials and copy words
make pictures and tell story of picture	refine fine motor skills develop oral language skills develop sequencing skills enrich vocabulary enhance oral communication	stimulate interest through attention and praise and encourage participation listen attentively and ask questions
write letters and make greeting cards	develop sequencing skills communicate through art communicate through print	provide materials draw out "exciting news," assist with letters and words act as scribe (if necessary)
make own books and discuss the book-making process	demonstrate an understanding of the function of print master book-handling skills	provide story patterns encourage creative thought act as scribe (if necessary)
keep a daily journal	communicate in print organize ideas develop spelling skills	provide a daily routine provide assistance as needed offer praise and encouragement
ask questions	analyze work of self/others	encourage creative thought develop reading comprehension

Capitalization

Teach beginning writers the basics of capitalization.

Get Ready

Talk to children about capitalization.
We use a capital letter to start a sentence:
    The dog was friendly.
    It is cold.

and when the person, place or thing we are writing about has a proper name:
    My friend's name is **J**ohn **P**eter **J**acobs.
    I attend **W**illowbrook **P**ublic **S**chool.
    I live in **C**arthage, **I**llinois.

We also use a capital whenever we write about ourselves using the word *I*.
    I feel happy when **I** am with my best friend.

(As children become more experienced writers, they can be introduced to other uses of capitalization.)

The dog was very friendly.

What to Do

1. Write several sentences of different construction on the chalkboard. Do not use any capitalization.
2. Go through each sentence and have the children indicate words that should begin with a capital letter.
3. Erase lowercase letters that require changing, and print the uppercase letters in different colors of chalk.

The girl's name is Patty.
A mouse lives in Texas.
Mr. Brown likes to sing.

One or More?

In this exercise, children learn about single and plural nouns.

Get Ready

Talk about the singular and plural forms.

When we write about something of which there is only one, we write the word in its singular form.
   One yellow **banana**.
When there are two or more of something, change the singular word to a plural. Plurals of most nouns are formed by often adding the letter "s."
   Two yellow **bananas**.
   A bunch of yellow **bananas**.

What to Do

Have the children print the singular or plural form of each word beneath its corresponding picture.

Punctuation Playtime

In this pop-up card game, children are introduced to punctuation.

Materials

✓ one set of period, question and exclamation marks (page 79)

Get Ready

Talk about the correct use of periods, question marks and exclamation points, using the punctuation cards as visual cues.

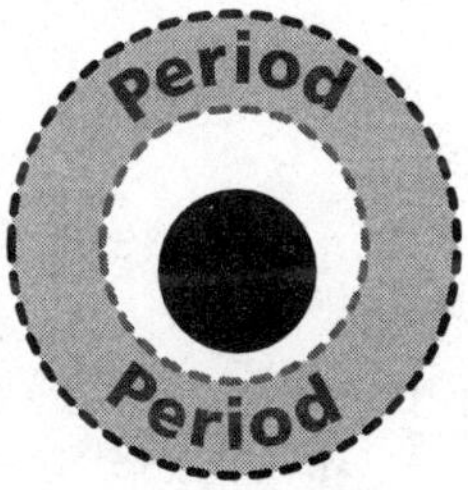

- A **period** is used to end a sentence that tells you what someone or something is or is not doing (makes a statement), tells you what to do (commands) or makes a request.

    Telling: I have a dog.
    Commanding: Do your homework.
    Requesting: Please help me with the dishes.

- A **question mark** is used to end a sentence that asks a direct question (an interrogative sentence) and to show doubt (questions **who**, **what**, **when**, **where**, **why** or **how**).

    Who was on the telephone?
    What are we having for dinner?
    Where did she go?
    When are we leaving?
    Why did he do that?
    How did you know who it was?

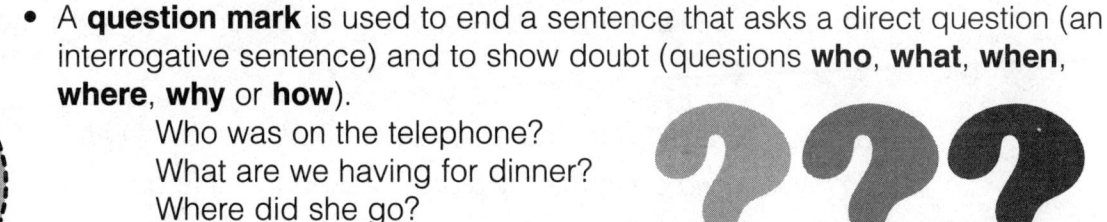

- An **exclamation point** is used to end a sentence that expresses excitement, surprise or another strong feeling.

    What a great day!
    It's you!
    Ouch!

Writing is fun to do!

How to Play

1. Sit in a circle with the children.
2. Distribute the punctuation cards. (The children should know in advance how each is used.)
3. Read a sentence aloud, using appropriate expression and inflection as auditory clues.
4. At the end of the sentence, have the children hold up a punctuation card.
5. Decide, as a group, which punctuation mark is the most appropriate.
   - Help! Somebody! Anybody! My house is on fire!
   - I went to my friend's birthday party. It was fun. We had cake and ice cream.
   - Would you like an apple for your snack? No? What about a banana?
   - Oh no! Is that the time? I'm late for dinner!

Try This

✓ Let the children make up sentences for their classmates to punctuate.
✓ Fill a sheet with unpunctuated sentences and photocopy for the class. As a seatwork exercise, read the sentences aloud and have the children hold up their punctuation cards. They can then print the correct punctuation on the sheet.
✓ Try this story. Pause at the end of each quote and each sentence. Wait for the children to raise their punctuation cards. The dialogue tags will provide the clues.

One day, a little girl went to the shopping mall with her mother.

"Mommy, can we go to the toy store?" asked the little girl.

"Of course!" said her mother.

They took the elevator down to the bottom floor of the mall. "Oh my, it's a long way down!" cried the little girl.

"Are you frightened?" asked the little girl's mother.

"A bit," said the little girl.

"Don't worry," said her mother. "We're almost there."

Soon, the elevator came to a stop. "Get ready! The doors are opening," said the little girl's mother.

When the doors opened, the little girl stepped out of the elevator and into the toy store.

"Look at all the toys!" she squealed. "Will you buy me one for being such a brave girl on the elevator?"

"You were awfully brave," said her mother. "Would you like a teddy bear to keep you company on the ride back up?"

"Oh yes!" cried the little girl. "Yes I would!"

Punctuation Playtime Cut-Outs

Photocopy, cut and enlarge the following punctuation marks for the Punctuation Playtime game on page 78. Laminate if desired. Each child will need one set of three: a period, question mark and exclamation point.

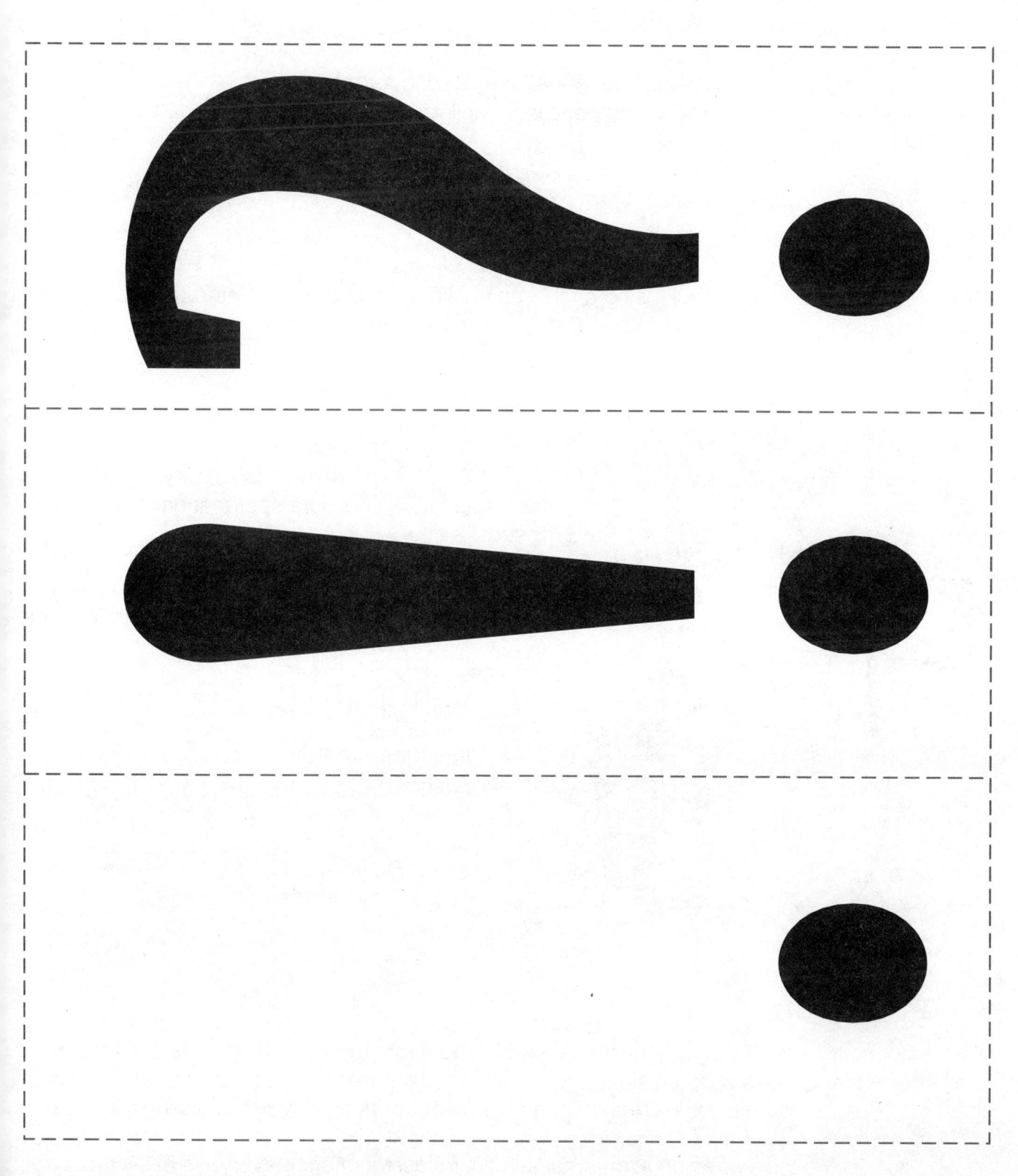

79

Simple Sign-Ins

Help young writers master an important printed word . . . their name!

Materials

- ✓ one large sign-in book
- ✓ name cards with each child's name if needed for reference
- ✓ fancy writing tools (flashy pencils, pencil grips, scented markers)

Get Ready

Make your sign-in book using chart paper, clip rings and a decorated tagboard cover, or use a simple scrapbook.

What to Do

1. Place the sign-in book in a spot that can't be missed.
2. Have children sign in when they arrive.
3. Write different titles on your sign-in page each day.
4. Add pictures to help children decipher the title of the day.

   Examples:
   Who Is Here?
   Our Class
   Fun Kids
   Friends
   Santa's Helpers
   Snow Kids
   Funny Bunnies
   The Sunshine Kids

Try This

- ✓ Some days you can make the sign-in into a pictograph to help collect valuable data. Have children sign or stick a happy face in the correct column to indicate age, mitten color, hair color, gender, number of pets, number of siblings and so on.
- ✓ Hang the sign-in book on a hook in your classroom once everyone has signed in.

Make a Greeting Card

Send a message while learning to read or write.

Materials

- ✓ paper strips with preprinted messages (for example: To, From, Love, Mom, Dad, Grandma, Grandpa, Happy Father's Day, Merry Christmas, Thank You, I Love You)
- ✓ construction paper to be folded into a card
- ✓ craft glue and glue sticks or brush
- ✓ writing instruments (pencils, crayons, markers, etc.)

What to Do

1. Prepare a sample card for reference.
2. Read the sample together.
3. Read the preprinted strips as a class. (You might want to have a competent reader on hand to assist emerging readers.)
4. Have children create their own greeting for someone special using materials at hand. Encourage children to use a combination for preprinted messages, their own handwritten messages and pictures to decorate the card.

Word Wishes

*In this whimsical creative art activity,
children are encouraged to express their wishes in words.*

Materials

- Word Wish Star Cut-Outs (below)
- pencils
- silver glitter
- string
- tape

What to Do

1. Give each child a "word wish" star.
2. Have the child print a wish on the blank side of the star.
3. Decorate the stars with silver glitter.
4. Tape string to the top of each star.
5. Hang the stars from the ceiling.

WORD WISH

Star light, star bright,
First star I see tonight,
I wish I may,
I wish I might
Have this wish,
I wish tonight.

Good News/Bad News

In this pro/con activity, children look for the good news in a bad news scenario, and discover that there are two sides to every coin, two sides to every argument and two ways to look at just about every situation.

Materials

✓ flip chart
✓ marker
✓ coin shape cut-outs (below)
✓ pencil
✓ tape
✓ string

What to Do

1. Write the following sentence starter on a number of pages in your flip chart: "The bad news is . . ."
2. With children in a group, brainstorm a bunch of bad situations.
3. Print each of these after a sentence starter on the flip chart pages.
4. Write the following positive sentence starter after each negative scenario: "The good news is . . ."
5. Choose one bad scenario and have the children think of as many "good" sides to the situation as they can.
6. Print each new response on the chart.
7. Do this for several or all of the scenarios.
8. Back at their desks, children can copy one of the scenarios from the board onto their coin cut-out, or create one of their own, printing the bad news on one side and the good news on the other.
9. Tape a piece of string to the top of each coin.
10. Hang the coins from the ceiling.

   Example: The bad news is . . . the dog ate my slippers.
          The good news is . . . I get a new pair of slippers!

Writing Folder

Create a personal writing folder for each child.

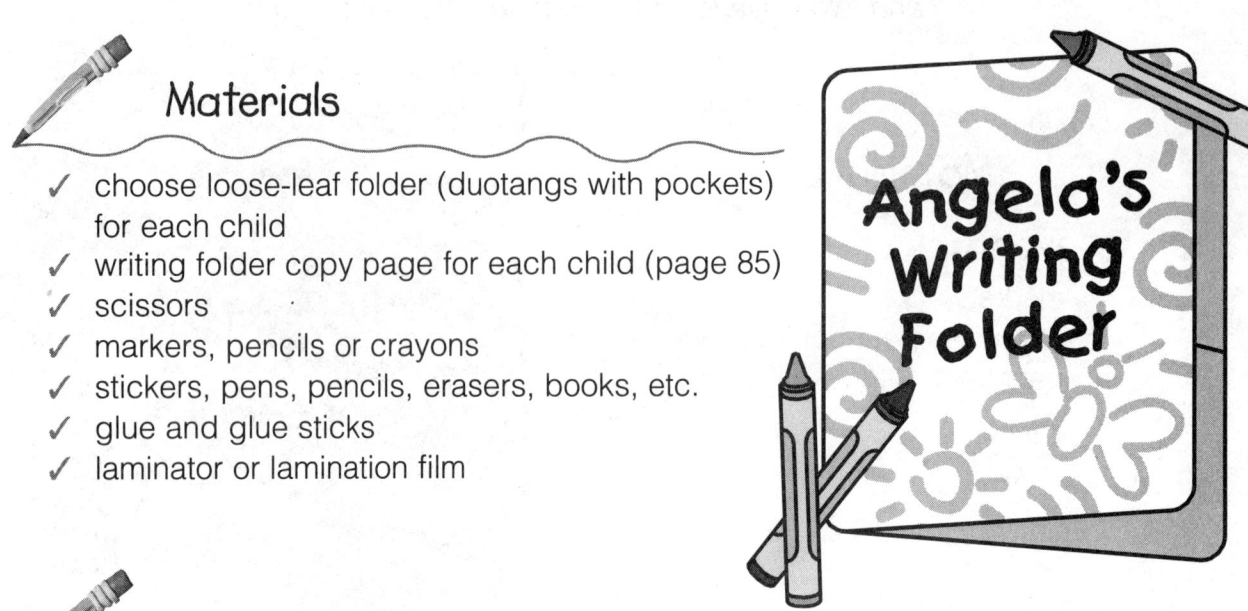

Materials

- ✓ choose loose-leaf folder (duotangs with pockets) for each child
- ✓ writing folder copy page for each child (page 85)
- ✓ scissors
- ✓ markers, pencils or crayons
- ✓ stickers, pens, pencils, erasers, books, etc.
- ✓ glue and glue sticks
- ✓ laminator or lamination film

What to Do

1. Have students cut on the dotted lines of the copy page.
2. Ask them to write their name on the line that reads _____'s Writing Folder. This title page should be glued to the front of the folder.
3. Have children paste the Grade 1 Writer's Checklist to the inside back cover of the folder.
4. When the glue has dried, have children decorate their folders.
5. Open up the folders, laminate and slit pocket with a craft knife. Use this pocket to store written work.

Using the Writing Folder

Provide each grade 1 student with a writing folder. This folder can be used to collect edited and unedited written works. Each piece should be date stamped for future reference. At the end of the year this folder can be sent home as a record of the young writer's progress.

_____'s

Writing Folder

Grade 1 Writing Folder

Just for Fun Writing (rough drafts)
- ❏ Write down my ideas.
- ❏ Sound out and spell the words as best I can.

From Rough Draft to Good Copy
- ❏ Read over my rough writing.
- ❏ Does it make sense?
- ❏ Did I use periods and capitals?
- ❏ Are all of the words spelled correctly?
- ❏ How does it look?
- ❏ Make changes.
- ❏ Make a good copy.

Sharing

A sharing classroom is a learning classroom!

The sharing of work, ideas and accomplishments provides intrinsic motivation for young writers as well as opportunities to reinforce old skills and develop new ones. Most children are very excited to share their work, and the experience helps them to develop both confidence and competence.

The sharing experience must be a positive one in which children receive reinforcement and praise from peers, educators, volunteers and parents. It should be a regular component of a language arts program. Children should be provided with many opportunities to share their new-found skills with others: reading and discussing their own work with educators, volunteers and parents; sharing their work in a group setting; displaying their work (on bulletin boards or in writing books that leave room for positive feedback and comments).

Develop a reading and writing culture in your class by encouraging dialogue about challenges, ideas and accomplishments. Sharing reinforces a child's new abilities and allows him to learn by example. The sharing of written works inspires children to be creative, thoughtful and thorough in expressing their thoughts in print.

Publish Your Work

Children enjoy the opportunity to take their writing to the final stage: publishing!

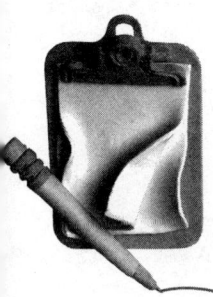

Set up a publishing center periodically throughout the school year. Publishing is exciting, but keep in mind that it is only one part of the writing process. It calls for fine editing and lots of assistance. While classroom focus should be on writing, it is exciting to give early writers the occasional opportunity to take short pieces of work to this final stage.

Try publishing these short works:

- ✓ lists and descriptions
- ✓ silly word collections
- ✓ weather word collection
- ✓ book of titles
- ✓ collection of letters
- ✓ jokes and riddles
- ✓ shape books and booklets
- ✓ fill-in-the-blank story pages and booklets

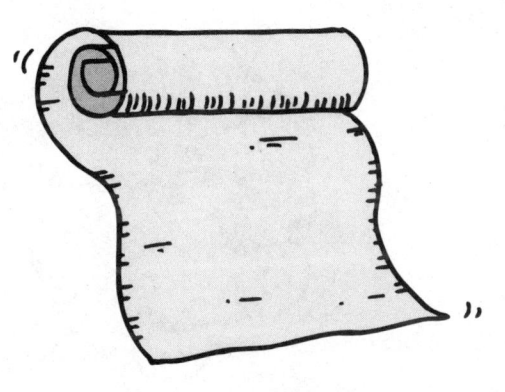

Try This

- ✓ Provide good quality paper and pencils for final copies.
- ✓ Produce final copies on the computer.
- ✓ Design a bulletin board to display finished works.
- ✓ Make a photocopied compilation of final products.
- ✓ Write on a scroll and roll it up.
- ✓ Decorate a cookie or cake with your story.
- ✓ Bind your story and cover it with fabric or a hard cover.
- ✓ Present the final copy in a shape book.
- ✓ Add real photographs to illustrate your story.
- ✓ Invite volunteer editors and bookmakers into your class.

Chapter 5

Story Makers

From Reading to Writing

Reading, writing and oral language communication are closely connected in child development. To create competent writers, educators must offer exciting reading experiences. Young children won't be experts, but through approximations and active learning, they can take part in the wonderful world of reading.

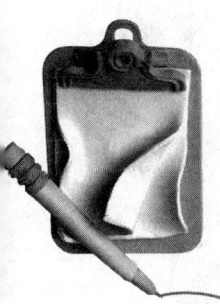

You can help children develop pre-reading and early reading skills in the following ways:

- ✓ Show enthusiasm for reading and an avid interest in printed materials.

- ✓ Demonstrate reading for pleasure and/or information.

- ✓ Read the daily calendar and weather report.

- ✓ Read "big books," large-print picture books, charts, lists, poems, songs and experience charts on a daily basis.

- ✓ Provide daily opportunities for children to read or mimic reading to another person (from symbols to sentences, anything counts!).

- ✓ Offer formal lessons in letter and sound awareness, word attack skills and cue and clue recognition.

- ✓ Provide access to large-print, easy-to-read and predictable materials.

- ✓ Make use of projectors and transparencies, computer stories and pocket charts.

- ✓ Prepare lessons focusing on consonant and vowel sounds.

- ✓ Offer word recognition activities.

- ✓ Provide exposure to an age-appropriate formal reading program.

Stories, Stories, Everywhere!

From the moment they wake up until the moment they go to bed, children's lives are filled with stories.

Think About It!

Help children identify the many sources of story in their lives.
- ✓ parents
- ✓ teachers
- ✓ relatives
- ✓ friends
- ✓ television and radio

What do children like about stories? Do they learn from them? Is it fun or entertaining just to listen? Do stories make them laugh, worry or get excited?

Invite a Storyteller

*Some of the best stories are in our minds, not in books.
Storytelling is a rich tradition that can both delight and inform children of all ages.*

We tell stories every day. Sometimes we tell stories about things that happened to us on the way to school or remember out loud the events of last week. Sometimes we pass on stories that we have heard from someone else. Sometimes we make up our own stories.

A long time ago, storytellers spread the news from town to town. Storytellers were a very important source of information and entertainment before people had newspapers, books or radios and televisions. Storytellers shared tales of adventure, survival, conflict and glory. They informed people of real events or entertained them with made-up stories that thrilled them or made them laugh or think.

Try to recapture history and your own heritage by inviting a professional storyteller to visit your group, or take on the role yourself to illustrate the oral tradition of storytelling. Show children that a story can be engaging without print or visual aids.

Circle Stories

Materials

✓ circle of children and a little imagination!
✓ pencil and paper (optional)

How to Play

1. Sit on the floor and have the children sit in a circle around you.
2. You start the story by saying, "Once upon a time . . ."
3. The child to your left builds on your story by finishing your incomplete sentence, " . . . there was a fairy princess" or ". . . a little brown cat got lost in the city" or ". . . I went to visit a mountain gorilla"–whatever! The sky is the limit with this creative and cooperative story-building game.
4. Play then passes to the left, with each child starting a sentence, adding a word or two to a sentence already in play, or finishing the sentence in play.
5. The game continues until the story comes to a "logical" conclusion or the children cannot build it any further. (It is helpful to periodically refresh the story in the minds of the children by repeating it from the beginning as best you can.)

Try This

✓ Have each child add only a single word to the sentence in play.
✓ Have each child add a complete sentence.
✓ Play the Secret Story Circle version of the game. To play, you will need a piece of paper and a pencil. You begin by whispering your story starter sentence into the ear of the child on your left. The child then whispers his sentence to you–from here on in, your job is to scribe for the children–and to the child on his left. That child then whispers her sentence to you and the person on her left. That child then whispers her sentence to you and the person on her left and so on, until one child (or you if it seems to be going nowhere or infinitely!) brings the story to an end. You then read the story out loud to the delight of all the children.

Say It with Pictures

Children can create a story without using words!

Materials

- blank booklet
- drawing instruments

Get Ready

1. Share a wordless picture book with your group.
2. Draw attention to the beginning, middle and end of the story.
3. Ask the leading question: "I wonder what will happen next?"
4. Encourage children to think about sequencing.

What to Do

1. Have children create their own wordless storybooks.
2. Have children pair off to share finished stories with their peers.

Try This

- Talk about pictures in a picture book. How do the pictures help to tell a story? Do you need to have words to make a story?

Picture Card Story Sequencers

In this cut-and-paste sequencing activity, children use their logic and reasoning skills to organize a series of related events. In the process, they will learn that stories, like most things we do, have a beginning, a middle and an end.

Materials

- six sets of Picture Card Stories, enlarged (pages 95-97)
- scissors
- blank pieces of paper (cut in thick strips)
- glue (or stapler)
- crayons, pencil crayons or markers

What to Do

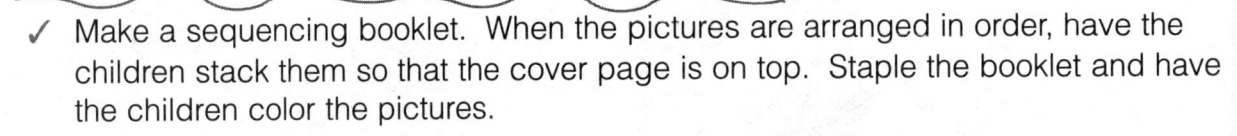

1. Give the children one strip of Picture Card Stories.
2. Have them cut the strip to make five different pictures.
3. Ask them to put the pictures in order, making sure that the sequence begins with the "cover" picture.
4. Keeping the pictures in order, have the child glue the "cover" picture at the top of the blank strip, roughly in the middle. Then paste the "story" pictures in a row below.
5. Have children color the story strip.

Try This

- Make a sequencing booklet. When the pictures are arranged in order, have the children stack them so that the cover page is on top. Staple the booklet and have the children color the pictures.

Picture Card Story Cut-Outs

The Drink

The Drink
- Child drinking juice
- Child opening fridge
- Child pouring juice

The Dog's Bone

The Dog's Bone
- Dog dropping bone in hole
- Dog digging hole in ground
- Dog getting bone from child

Picture Card Story Cut-Outs

The Butterfly's Story

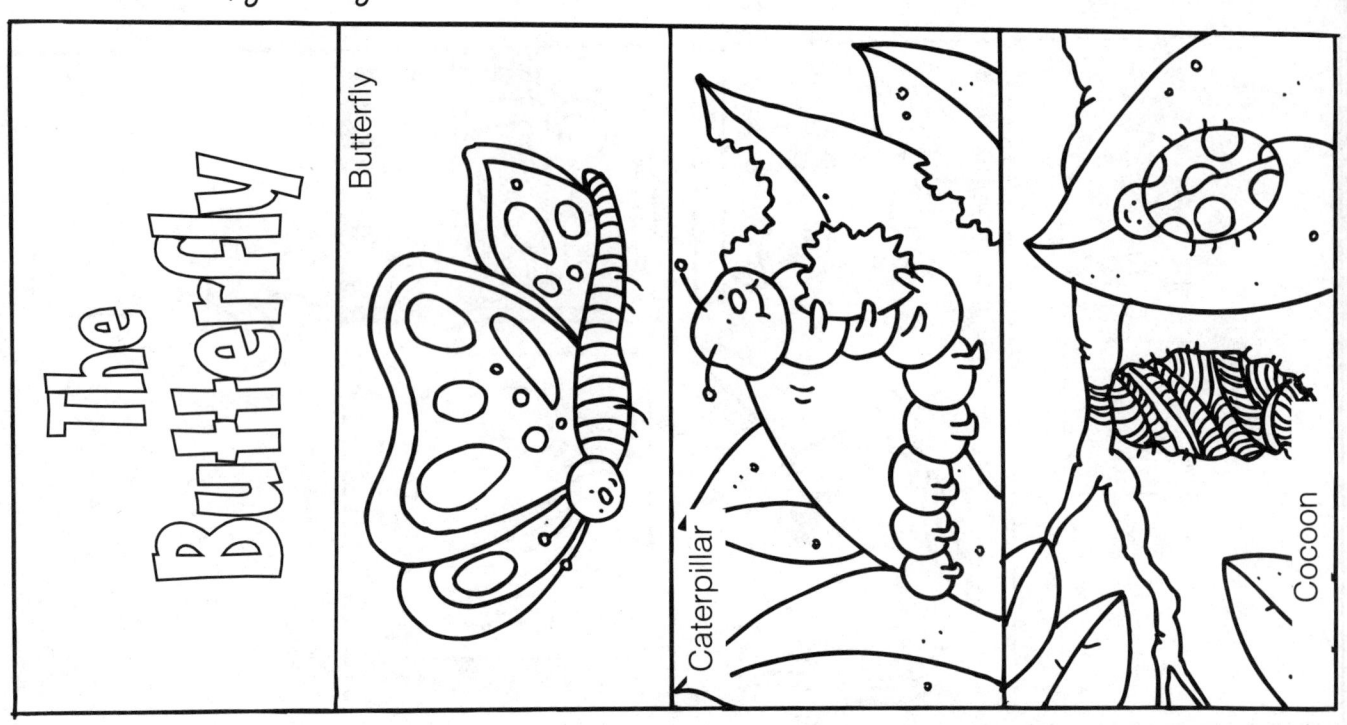

The Butterfly | Butterfly | Caterpillar | Cocoon

The Camping Trip

THE CAMPING TRIP | Sleeping in tent | Setting up tent. | Driving in car with camping gear on roof

96

TLC10201 Copyright © Teaching & Learning Company, Carthage, IL 62321-00

# Picture Card Story Cut-Outs

Growing Flowers

Growing Flowers | Picking a flower | Watering the plants | Planting seeds in the ground

Bedtime

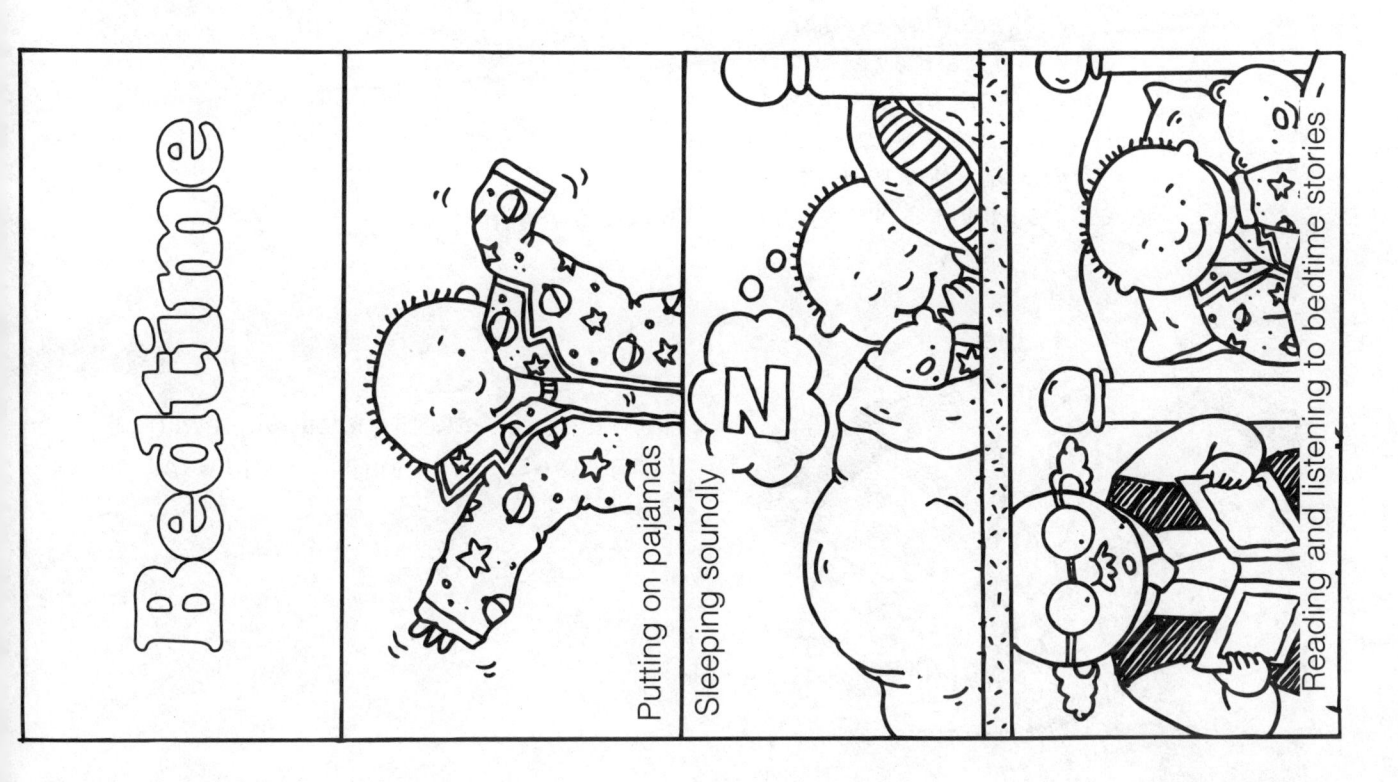

Bedtime | Putting on pajamas | Sleeping soundly | Reading and listening to bedtime stories

Story Box

Illustrations serve as context clues for reading and play an integral role in storytelling.

Materials

✓ story box (shoe box decorated with exciting pictures)
✓ story idea picture cards

Get Ready

Compile a collection of pictures that tell a story.

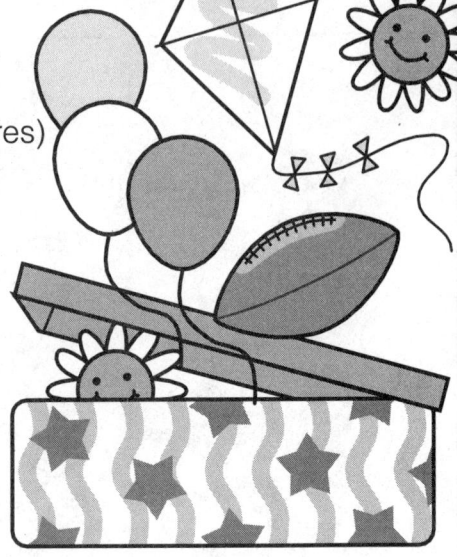

What to Do

1. Choose one pair of students to choose a story idea from the box.
2. Help the students to analyze the picture before telling the story. Use questions to provoke thought. For example:
   Who are these people?
   What are they doing?
   Where are they?
   When did this happen?
   Why are they doing this?
   How are they feeling?
3. Have a pair tell the class a story about the picture.

Try This

✓ Have the pair act out the situation without using words. Can the group figure out what is going on?

Scribe a Story

Children are authors of wonderful stories long before they are able to write. Parents and educators can encourage this creativity by acting as "scribes" and putting a child's thoughts into words. Making written notation of a child's ideas not only facilitates and captures the imagination of the young author but also helps to inspire a love of storytelling that will last a lifetime.

Materials

- ✓ child with a desire to "write"
- ✓ scribe's undivided attention
- ✓ time
- ✓ computer or writing paper and pencil/pen

What to Do

1. Take the child to a quiet spot where he can concentrate.
2. If the child does not have an idea for a story, provide some ideas. Encourage her to tell you everything that comes to mind.
3. Write or type everything that the child tells you. Don't worry about spelling, punctuation and sentence structure. The important thing is to get ideas down on paper.
4. After the child has finished dictating, put in the appropriate punctuation and read the work out loud.
5. Ask if there is anything he would like to change or expand.
6. Find out if she would like to make any pictures to accompany her story.
7. Print a good copy of the story. Make sure there are not too many words on each page. If there are to be illustrations, leave space on each page for a picture.
8. Display the story where the child can see his work. Send it to school if you are a parent scribe or home if you are the child's classroom teacher or helper.

Silly Sentences

In this hilarious creative thinking game that introduces sentence structure and reinforces reading, sequencing, numbering and even adding skills, kids learn that all writing is good writing–especially when it's silly!

Materials

- ✓ piece of tagboard divided into Silly Sequence grid (page 102)
- ✓ marker
- ✓ two dice
- ✓ three game pieces or place markers
- ✓ Silly Sentences Flip-Up Books (page 101)

Get Ready

	Who?	Did What?	Where?

1. Turn the tagboard so that it is taller than it is wide.
2. Make three vertical lines down the length of the board, dividing it into four columns. (The first column will be very narrow.)
3. Draw 12 evenly spaced horizontal lines across the board, making 52 boxes.
4. Leave the top left box empty.
5. In the top box (second from the left), print the word *WHO?*
6. In the top box (third from the left), print the words *DID WHAT?*
7. In the top right box, print the word *WHERE?*
8. Your grid is now ready for mounting.

What to Do

1. Have the children provide you with enough WHO?s, DID WHAT?s, WHERE?s to fill the grid. (See the Silly Sentences Sample Grid on page 102.) Stick to one gender and use only the pronouns *he/his* or *she/her*. Using them interchangeably does not work. (*My, I, our* and *we* are fine to use.)
2. After the grid is complete, have the children take turns rolling the dice. After the first roll, ask the child to determine the sum of the two dice and place a marker on the WHO? space that corresponds to that sum in the number column. Do the same for the second and third rolls, placing a marker on the DID WHAT? and WHERE? spaces.
3. When each column has a marker in it, choose a child to read the silly sentence.
4. When the laughter has subsided, remove the markers and begin a new round.

Silly Sentences Flip-Up Book

- ✓ To make a Silly Sentences Flip-Up Book, copy the Silly Sentences Grid onto an 8 1/2" x 11" (22 x 28 cm) sheet of paper, omitting the numbers 1-12.
- ✓ Photocopy the grid so that you have one sheet for every child.
- ✓ Cut the grid across the rows so that you have 13 vertical strips of paper. (The WHO? DID WHAT? WHERE? strip will be the cover page.)
- ✓ Assemble the Silly Sentences Flip-Up Book by layering the 13 strips on top of one another in any order. (The cover strip must be on top.)
- ✓ Attach the strips by stapling horizontally across the top.
- ✓ Make vertical cuts in the strips between the WHO? DID WHAT? WHERE? columns. Be sure not to cut all the way to the top.
- ✓ To make a silly sentence, flip up a different number of pages in each column.

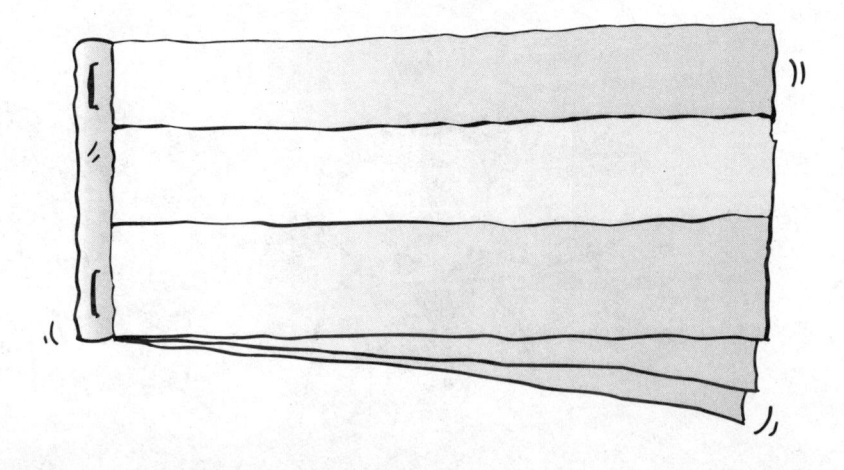

Silly Sentences Sample Grid

	WHO?	DID WHAT?	WHERE?
1.	The king	spilled water	on the throne.
2.	My dad	dropped a jar	on the floor.
3.	Susan's dog	buried a bone	in our garden.
4.	The supervisor	gave a detention	in the yard.
5.	Our priest	said a special prayer	in church.
6.	The T-Rex	killed a raptor	in the Jurassic Period.
7.	The principal	started yelling	over the P.A. system.
8.	The teacher	read a story	in circle.
9.	My pet lizard	ate a mouse	in the terrarium.
10.	A police officer	arrested a bad guy	at the store.
11.	My doctor	took my temperature	in my mouth.
12.	A horse	bucked a cowboy	into the dirt.

Story Lovers' Club

Children love stories. They love to listen to stories, to share stories and to write stories. This love of language can be promoted and enjoyed in a multifaceted educational program we call the Story Lovers' Club.

The Story Lovers' Club encourages children to further their love of stories and storytelling and to develop their reading, writing and oral language skills in a fun, friendly and socially stimulating environment. The club can meet weekly, monthly or just once a year, and it can be structured as a classroom activity that is incorporated in the regular curriculum or organized as an extracurricular activity hosted over a lunch hour.

Although the possibilities for Story Lovers' Club activities are limitless, a number of "starter" ideas are described on the following pages.

Share a Story
Club organizers can bring stories to share or encourage club members to bring their favorite stories from home. These can be read out loud and used as a springboard for dialogue and discussion.

Discuss a Favorite Story
Each child is asked in advance to bring a favorite story to a club meeting. The child gives a brief account of the story to club members, shows his favorite illustration and gives reasons why the story is his favorite. (Time permitting, these stories can be read out loud.)

Illustrate a Story

Children are encouraged to listen to a story and then draw pictures to illustrate it. This can be a single or group activity.

- ✓ Children may choose to draw a single picture to illustrate a specific event or a series of pictures to represent the entire story.
- ✓ Each child can be assigned one page to illustrate. These pictures can then be used to produce a Story Lovers' Club version of the book.
- ✓ A large piece of paper can be mounted in the classroom or on an outside wall to be colored or painted by club members.
- ✓ Using a large sheet of paper, members can work cooperatively to illustrate one picture, each child in turn adding a single further detail to the picture.

Crafty Stories

Plan a related craft as a follow-up activity to the reading of a favorite story.

Snack Time Stories

Prepare a snack for sharing that is featured in a story.

Lunch Box Stories

Have each child bring a story from home that fits into a lunch box or bag. Read the stories aloud while the children eat their lunch.

Story Animators

Select a story that has been animated and is available on video.

- ✓ Read the story to club members and then show the video.
- ✓ Discuss similarities and differences.
- ✓ Discuss preferences.
- ✓ Read another book, preferably by the same author and in the same series. Decide what would have to go in the video and what could be left out. Should anything be changed? Why?
- ✓ What books would the club members like to see animated?
- ✓ Write a letter to the publisher and video production company expressing the children's desire to see the book in video format.

Story Builders

This is a fun and easy way to give the club members a chance to express their ideas in story format.

- ✓ With the children sitting in a circle in front of a chalkboard or flip chart, write out a story starter: "Once upon a time . . ." or "The other day . . ." or "When I was just little . . ." etc.
- ✓ Then have each child in turn add another complete thought to the story. (Older children might like to leave sentence "danglers" instead of complete thoughts. For example: Once upon a time . . . I found a little puppy in a deserted alley. He was so . . .dirty that I couldn't even tell what color he was. I took him home and . . .)
- ✓ Continue to build the story until everyone has had at least one turn; then bring it to a logical conclusion, either with a child's sentence or one of your own.
- ✓ Before the next club meeting, make a good copy of the story and photocopy one for every child. If you would like the children to illustrate the story, make sure your layout leaves lots of room for pictures. "Publishing" the story by laminating each child's copy would make a nice gift at the final club meeting.

Featured Author Day

Select a favorite author, one who has written a number of books for young children.

- ✓ Read a selection of these stories (or passages from each). Talk about the author's style and approach to story writing.
- ✓ Choose a favorite story.
- ✓ Write a letter to the author telling him/her how much club members enjoy his/her stories.
- ✓ Contact the author's publisher in advance of a feature day. Publishers will occasionally contribute to this kind of event, supplying such gratuitous items as bookmarks and even books.

Featured Illustrator Day

This activity follows the same outline as the Featured Author Day, but the focus is on the pictures rather than the text.

Special Guest/Special Reader Day

✓ Contact a local author or illustrator to see if he or she is willing to spend an hour with your club. (While many published authors charge a fee for such visits, some are quite willing to donate their time to a worthy cause.) There are lots of authors in every community who have not yet had the good fortune to be published. These hard-working and talented people often have dozens of unpublished but excellent works they are willing to share with eager audiences.

✓ Write a letter to parents, students in older grades, siblings of club members, high school and university coop students–anybody who might be a willing and interested reader–and ask them to share a story of their choosing with your club. To show your appreciation, you could even offer them an honorary membership in your club!

✓ Always send visitors a thank-you note on behalf of the children in the club. Make sure you mention the title of the book they shared with the group. (If you have some keen and capable writers in your group, ask them to write the notes.

Library Day

Take the club to the school or local library.

✓ See if the librarian is available to take the children on a short tour and then read them a story. (Some will even provide a craft or a snack.)

✓ If this is a lunchtime trip, try to book a room in which the children can eat. The children could choose a few books from the library, and you could bring these into the room to read while they munch their lunch.

✓ If possible, and with parents' permission, have the children apply for a library card–and perhaps even borrow a book or two! (If this is not an option, let the children select some books for you to borrow. These can be savored at your next Story Lovers' Club meeting.)

Story Lenders

At one (or each) meeting, have club members bring in a story that they are willing to "lend" to another club member. Keep a "Lenders' List" so that you can keep track of who borrowed what from whom and when it is returned. Because of the nature of the this activity, it might be wise to send a letter home soliciting parental approval beforehand.

Story Exchange

Have each club member bring in one "old" story to exchange for a "new" one. To make sure that the exchange is fair and that all participants have an opportunity to give and receive a book, you might want to put each club member's name on a slip of paper and place them in a hat. Each child then draws a name and takes the book from the person indicated on the slip. As an alternative, you could place all the books in a garbage bag and have children select a book from the bag. (In the interest of subject matter, boys and girls can be separated into two different drawings for both of these exchange options. You can, of course, simply let children exchange books with whomever they want. To eliminate any risk of disappointment, make sure you have several books on hand that you are willing to exchange.

Secondhand Story Sale

Have the children collect or donate used books for a Secondhand Story Sale. You can have an announcement published in the school newsletter or community paper. Make sure the event is well advertised. Proceeds from the sale can be used to purchase new books for the club or the school library, to finance a special excursion or can be donated to a worthwhile literacy cause.

Sandwich Stories

- ✓ Copy Sandwich Story Cut-Outs (page 108) onto colored paper. There should be enough cut-outs for each child to have a complete set. (The bread slice must be copied twice for each child. One slice will be used for the cover page, the other reserved for "The End.")
- ✓ Create a short story as a group (see Story Builders on page 105), or re-create a familiar one. (If the children are more advanced in their writing skills, they can be encouraged to develop their own stories. Interested children can be given extra "ingredients" to make another Sandwich Story at home.)
- ✓ Use one slice of bread for the cover; reserve the other for "The End."
- ✓ Have children print the body of the story on the other sandwich ingredients in any order they desire.
- ✓ Staple the sandwich together.

Sandwich Story Cut-Outs

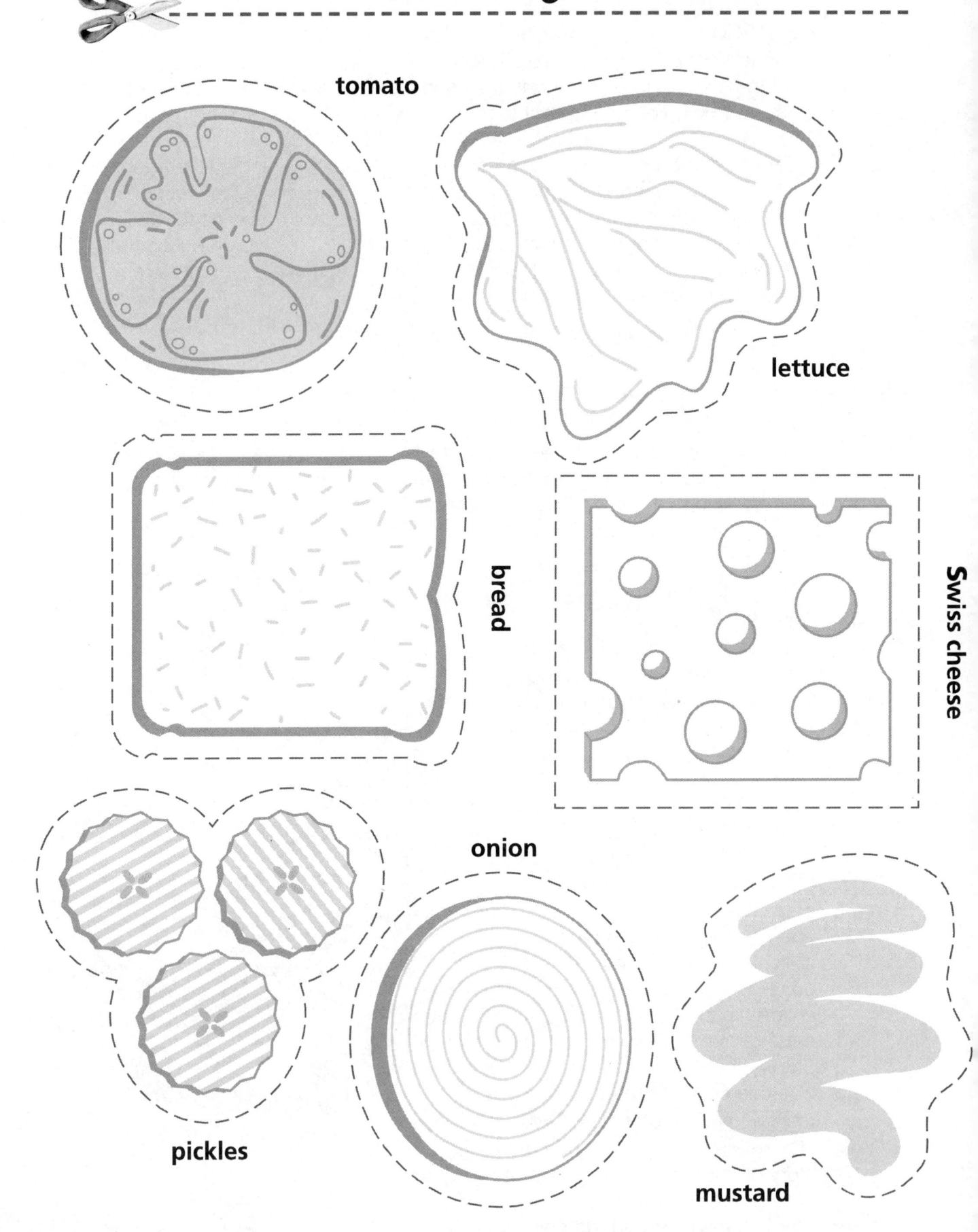

tomato

lettuce

bread

Swiss cheese

onion

pickles

mustard

Dear Story Lover!

You are invited to join a very special club ... the Story Lovers' Club!

Are you a book lover?
Do you like listening to stories, telling stories or reading stories?
Do stories take you to new spaces and exciting places and introduce you to strange, new faces?
Would you like to share awesome reading adventures with your friends?

If you answered "yes" to any of these questions,
the Story Lovers' Club is the place for you!

Join us on _____

at

in _____
for some fact, fiction, fantasy, fast action and fun!

Can't wait to see you there!

P.S. Please bring along a friend and one of your favorite stories

Story Lovers' Club
Official Membership Badge

Dear Story Lovers' Club member,

Here is your very own, official,
Story Lovers' Club Membership Badge!

Please color your badge and ask a grown-up to help you to cut it out.

You can bring your badge to Story Lovers' Club meetings
or even ask a grown-up to pin it to your shirt!

Welcome to the Club!

STORY LOVERS' CLUB
Membership Badge
member name

Chapter 6

Just for Fun

Imagination Station

Offer students a place to let their creativity take root and lead their pens and pencils in drawing and writing activities. An Imagination Station is an oasis for creativity–right in the classroom.

What to Do

1. Provide an ever-changing array of stimulating activities at an "Imagination Station."
2. Offer a setting that is relaxing and exciting all at once. You can provide pillows, beanbag chairs, interesting desks and chairs.
3. If possible, separate this area from the busy happenings of the classroom.
4. Consider a piano, bookcase, hanging curtains or beads as a barrier.
5. Provide relevant music, table coverings, textures, mobiles, chimes or other sensory stimuli.
6. Invite creative minds to explore!

Try This

✓ Make this center the first where new writing tools are introduced. Consider the wide array of vibrant markers with scented and shaped tips to inspire imaginations.

✓ Turn a new scrapbook into an imagination journal. This book will contain the creative end products of a variety of Imagination Station activities. Have children record their imaginings in squiggles, drawings or words.

Spread the News

With this useful recording and sharing tool, children learn that we use writing to convey information and to "record history"–and to give and offer praise and congratulations!

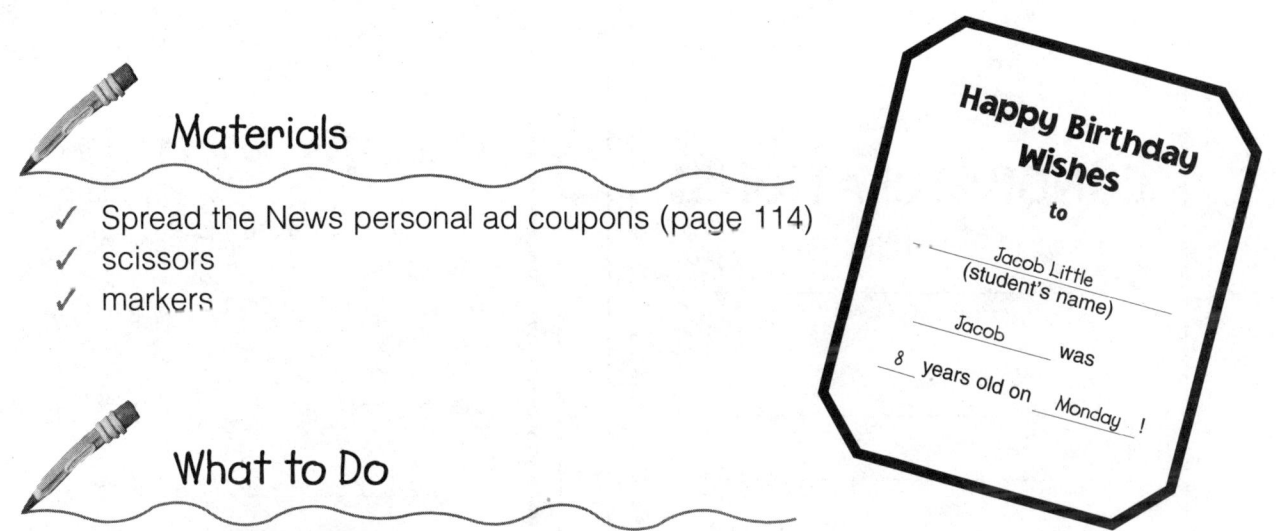

Materials

- ✓ Spread the News personal ad coupons (page 114)
- ✓ scissors
- ✓ markers

> **Happy Birthday Wishes**
> to
> _Jacob Little_
> (student's name)
> _Jacob_ was _8_ years old on _Monday_ !

What to Do

1. Use the "Personal Ads" on the Spread the News coupon page to celebrate special occasions–a lost tooth, a new baby at home, a birthday, a great result in sports, a good effort, etc.
2. Photocopy the Spread the News cut-out page, cut out the ad coupons and enlarge if desired.
3. When you want to recognize a child or make an announcement on his behalf, just transfer the details onto a personal ad coupon.
4. Staple these coupons on a special bulletin board or around the classroom.
5. Make a copy of the coupon for the child to take home.
6. Compile the coupons and include a "personals" page in your monthly newsletter to parents.

Spread the News

CONGRATULATIONS!

_____
(student's name)

You _____

_____

_____!
(describe event, achievement,
or occasion)

Happy Birthday Wishes

to

_____
(student's name)

_____ was

_____ years old on _____!

WOW!

Today, _____
(student's name)

_____

_____

_____!
(describe achievement)

Extra! Extra! Read All About It!

_____
(student's name)

_____

_____

_____!
(describe accomplishment/acquisition)

And we're going to shout it!

The Magic Looking Glass

Look through the magic looking glass. What do you see?

Materials

- ✓ The Magic Looking Glass copy page (page 116)
- ✓ large magnifying glass
- ✓ interesting things for magnification
- ✓ kaleidoscopes
- ✓ paper
- ✓ pencils, crayons and markers

What to Do

1. Encourage children to visit a Magic Looking Glass Center in the classroom and look through the magnifying glasses.
2. Ask them to describe what they see.
3. Have them look through the kaleidoscope. What does the pattern look like? Draw and color a kaleidoscope picture of a blank piece of paper.
4. Talk about what you might see if you looked through a magic looking glass.
5. On the copy page, have children draw and/or write about their "vision" inside the looking glass shape provided.

Name _____

The Magic Looking Glass

Look through the magic looking glass. What do you see?

What Will Grow from the Magic Beans?

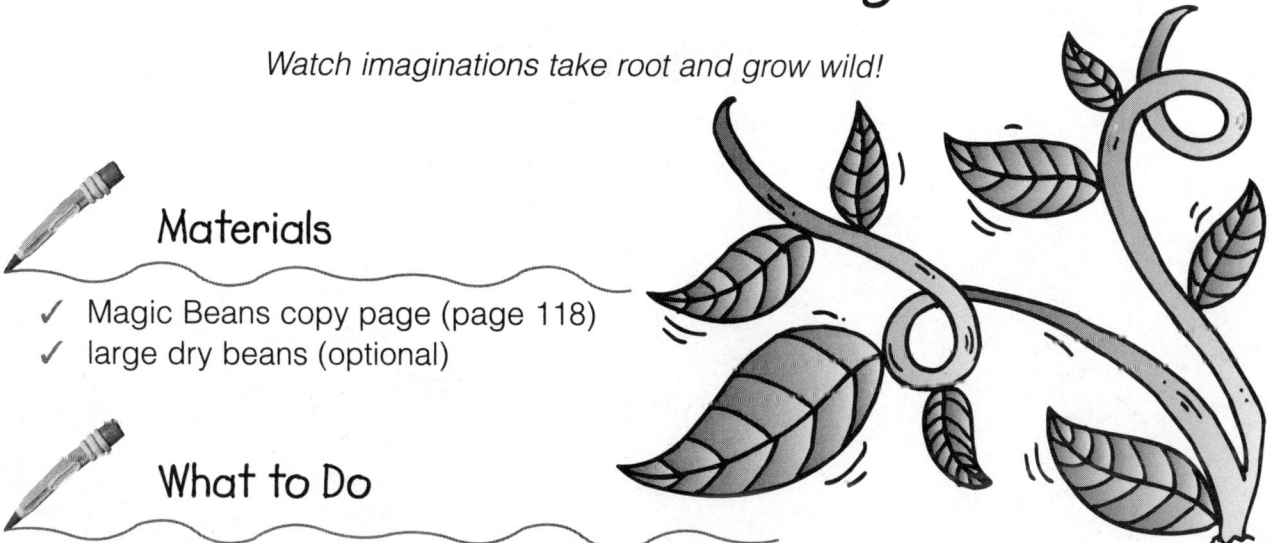

Watch imaginations take root and grow wild!

Materials

- ✓ Magic Beans copy page (page 118)
- ✓ large dry beans (optional)

What to Do

1. Have children paste bean shapes or decorate the bean shapes with various craft materials or coloring tools.
2. Let children's imaginations take root as their ideas sprout into drawings that fill the page.

Name _____

Magic Beans

What will grow from your magic beans?

Who Wore These?

Materials

- ✓ collection of interesting shoes and boots
- ✓ drawing paper
- ✓ pencils, erasers, pencil crayons or markers

What to Do

1. Put a pair of shoes or boots in a place of honor at the Imagination Station.
2. Have the children visit the center and look over the footwear.
3. Ask the children to draw a picture of the person–or thing!–that might have worn the shoes or boots.

What's Inside?

Shh!

Materials

- ✓ large box wrapped in plain brown paper and taped with masking tape
- ✓ butcher string to tie the package
- ✓ markers, pencils and other writing tools

What to Do

1. Make a sign that reads: *What's Inside?* Tape the sign to the box top.
2. Have children think about what might be inside the package.
3. Have children draw illustrations or write descriptions on the box to reveal what they think might be hiding inside.

What Would They Say?

In these activities, children use pictures and puppets to generate spontaneous dialogue.

Picture Talk

Materials

- ✓ box of pictures (animals and people)

What to Do

1. Working in pairs, have each child pull a picture from the box.
2. Put the pictures side by side.
3. What would the people/animals in the pictures say to one another?

Puppet Talk

Materials

- ✓ puppet stage
- ✓ puppets

How to Play

1. Set up a puppet stage.
2. Provide some puppets.
3. With children in pairs, have them choose a puppet and put on a little play. They can make up their dialogue as they go.

Try This

- ✓ See if the pairs of children would like to put on their play for the class.
- ✓ Once the children have had an opportunity to explore the puppet play area, introduce situations that the puppet might encounter (going back in time, losing a puppy, going to a restaurant, having a birthday party). How do the children (and the puppets) respond to these situations?

BYOS (Bring Your Own Senses) Party

*Overload your senses at this super stimulating
touching, tasting, seeing, smelling and hearing party.*

Materials

- ✓ five labeled sensory tables: Terrific Tasters, Touchy Feelers, Super Sniffers, Sightseers and Ear Piercers
- ✓ at each table a variety of different sensory delights to be experienced and described: tastes (Terrific Tasters), textures (Touchy Feelers), smells (Super Sniffers), sights (Sightseers) and sounds (Ear Piercers)
- ✓ paper
- ✓ pencils

Terrific Tasters   **Touchy Feelers**    **Super Sniffers**    **Sightseers**    **Ear Piercers**

What to Do

1. Set up sensory tables before the children arrive at school. (You will want to invite parent helpers to send in sensory items, to help with setup and cleanup, to man the tables during the activity and to write down children's observations. Make sure of any allergies in advance, and exclude potentially dangerous items from the tables.)
2. Divide the children into five groups. They will move from table to table in their assigned groups.
3. Give children about 10 minutes at each table. Have them experience the objects on the table with the appropriate sense, and then describe the experience to the parent "scribes." They can use single words, phrases or complete sentences.
4. Make a BYOS booklet. Have the children pick their favorite item from each table and draw it. They can use the corresponding sensory list to copy a number of descriptions for each item.

Appendix

Kindergarten Writing Readiness Assessment Form

Name _____

Expectations	Achievement Level	Comments
Fine Motor Development		
Holds pencil or drawing instruments		
Colors within the lines		
Traces letters and numbers		
Mimics writing behaviors		
Print, Letter and Word Awareness		
Recognizes letters		
Can say alphabet		
Recognizes name		
Matches upper- and lowercase letters		
Uses left to right print analysis		
Recognizes numbers to 20		
Possesses a simple sight vocabulary		
Recognizes beginning sounds		
Recognizes ending sounds		

Achievement Level Key
1. Demonstrates independent, consistent mastery of skill or understanding of concept.
2. Demonstrates mastery of skill or understanding of concept most of the time.
3. Demonstrates a limited mastery of skill or understanding of concept with assistance.
4. Needs further assistance to acquire skill or understand concept.

Kindergarten Writing Readiness Assessment Form continued

Name _____

Expectations	Achievement Level	Comments
Word Usage		
Uses words appropriately for developmental level		
Internalizes new words		
Organization		
Expresses ideas with clarity		
Communicates ideas through drawings		
Organizes simple ideas into proper sequence		
Dictates a story		
Brings creativity and life experiences to stories		
Writing		
Makes use of various tools and mediums for making letters		
Is aware that words have a beginning, middle and ending sound		
Prints own name, letters of the alphabet, numerals to 10 and some familiar words		
Copies or creates symbols, pictures and words for specific purposes		
Enjoys writing		

LC10201 Copyright © Teaching & Learning Company, Carthage, IL 62321-0010

Grade 1 Writing Assessment Form

Name _____

Expectations	Achievement Level	Date Achieved
Understanding of Print, Letters and Words		
recognizes all letters and letter sounds		
uses left to right print analysis		
possesses a simple sight vocabulary		
recognizes beginning, middle and ending sounds		
Word Usage		
uses familiar words		
recognizes proper word order		
uses sound patterns such as rhyme		
experiments with new and imaginative words		
conveys ideas with clarity and expression		
Use of Writing		
develops ideas in print		
communicates greetings, ideas, thoughts and feelings through drawings		
uses print for specific purposes		
uses symbols, drawings, letters and words to convey messages		
brings experiences and knowledge of the outside world to written work		

Grade 1 Writing Assessment Form continued

Expectations	Achievement Level	Date Achieved
Organization of Ideas		
organizes simple ideas into proper sequence		
plans information to convey a clear message		
produces short pieces of writing using simple forms (stories, descriptions, lists of information)		
revises simple pieces of writing with assistance		
uses various strategies to sound out and spell unfamiliar words		
Conventions and Mechanics		
knows all of the consonant and long and short vowel sounds		
writes simple, complete sentences		
forms the plural of one-syllable words		
understands the use of the period and comma		
uses capital letters to begin sentences and identify names, places and the pronoun *I*		
recognizes and spells familiar words		
Visual Presentation		
prints legibly		
makes use of space between words		
enhances presentation with illustrations, etc.		

Achievement Level Key
1. Demonstrates independent, consistent mastery of skill or understanding of concept.
2. Demonstrates mastery of skill or understanding of concept most of the time.
3. Demonstrates a limited mastery of skill or understanding of concept with assistance.
4. Needs further assistance to acquire skill or understand concept.

Stages of Writing Development Checklist

There is a particular, predictable sequence of writing development. Dated observations and samples will help chart each child's progress.

Child's Name: _____

Stage 1: Scribbling
Date:

Stage 2: Early Line Drawings
Date:

Stage 3: Pre-Letter Shapes
Date:

Stage 4: Early Letters/Word Approximations
Date:

Stage 5: Invented Spelling
Date:

Stage 6: Standard Spelling
Date: